Flora Annie Steel

Books by
VIOLET POWELL

Autobiographical

Five out of Six
Within the Family Circle

General

A Substantial Ghost
The Irish Cousins
A Compton-Burnett Compendium
Margaret, Countess of Jersey
Flora Annie Steel, Novelist of India

Flora Annie Steel

NOVELIST OF INDIA

Violet Powell

HEINEMANN : LONDON

William Heinemann Ltd
10 Upper Grosvenor Street,
London W1X 9PA
LONDON MELBOURNE TORONTO
JOHANNESBURG AUCKLAND

First published 1981

434 59957 3

Printed and bound in Great Britain
by Mackays of Chatham

To the late

SIR MORTIMER WHEELER,
C.H., C.I.E., M.C.

in memory of travels through the Indian sub-continent

Contents

List of Illustrations

Nos. 2, 3, 4, 5, 6, 7, 8, 10 and 11 are reproduced by kind permission of the India Office Library and Records. No. 15 was kindly supplied by Mrs Gillian Hunting Simpson.

Introduction and Acknowledgements

Flora Annie Steel died on April 12th, 1929, ten days after her eighty-second birthday. At about this date I first read *On the Face of the Waters*, increasingly fascinated by the world which Mrs Steel painted in such strong colours. Being brought up not only on Kipling, but on a quantity of children's books of Indian background, this world had never been entirely strange to me. *On the Face of the Waters* did, however, shed a new light on a landscape of which some features had remained to me mysterious.

More than forty years later, my husband and I stayed in the country house at Farringford in the Isle of Wight which had once been the home of Alfred, Lord Tennyson. The house is now an hotel, but, as Robert Conquest wrote in a poem: "Beautiful! Unchanged in mood." I hope I may be excused for quoting from the diary I was keeping on that Island holiday.

Writing in Tennyson's Library (and now television room) October 1971: "The rain came down in sheets and A.T.'s ghost wailed in the hall, at least that's what it sounded like . . . I have been enthralled with *On the Face of the Waters* by Flora Annie Steel. I think (later writers) owe a lot to her technique of inspired hindsight." This is a reference to the undercover activities of Jim Douglas. A brilliant chap, with feet in all camps, he sees exactly how to avert the disaster of the Mutiny, but is prevented by mischance from influencing the course of history. The diary continues: "I came near to tears over Hodson and the Princes at Humayun's tomb, and the scenes in the private audience hall in the Red Fort, where I have twice had the pleasure of writing down 'If there is a Paradise on earth' . . ." I omitted the famous ending of the inscription, "It is here, It is here, It is here", which, on two visits to Delhi, I had faithfully copied into my sketchbook-diary.

xi

After this second reading of *On the Face of the Waters*, I do not think that I had the immediate idea of writing about its author. But as books and television programmes on the subject of the British in India became ever more popular, the debt that many of them owed to Mrs Steel became increasingly clear. My imagination was stirred. I began to read more of her books, finding her autobiography, *The Garden of Fidelity*, an encouragement to look farther into her life as a writer, an educationalist and a supporter of Votes for Women. I found her vitality to have been unflagging in all these fields. I was also struck by the prodigality of her invention, which always made me wish to know what, in her stories, was going to happen next. This secret of a good teller of tales was one to which Flora Annie Steel had the key. If others, to whom her books are unknown, can be encouraged to explore the world she made so peculiarly hers, the following study will have been justified.

I must express my gratitude to Mr Neil Webster, surviving grandson of Flora Annie Steel. He and Mrs Webster kindly entertained me in their home, when they discussed Mrs Steel's life and character. Additionally, Mr Webster drew my attention to Mrs Daya Patwardhan's invaluable book *A Star of India*. Besides sorting out the ramifications of the Steel and Webster families, Mr Webster was also kind enough to show me such material as remained in his possession, his grandmother having burnt the bulk of her papers when writing *The Garden of Fidelity*. I must, however, emphasize that statements of opinion or interpretation of facts are mine alone.

This also applies to such information as was kindly given me by Colonel Greville Steel, great-nephew of Henry Steel, the husband of Flora Annie Steel.

Mrs Mildred Archer, of the India Office Library, has, by her sympathy and encouragement, been a strong support throughout the writing of this book. The staff of the India Office Library has been unfailingly helpful. In particular, Mrs Katharine Bell took immense trouble to track down suitable illustrations.

Mr Edgar Hyde was kind enough to lend me E. F. Oaten's *Anglo-Indian Literature*, valuable for a contemporary view of Flora Annie Steel's writing.

Mr Roland Gant, of William Heinemann Ltd, has made my work far less arduous than it would otherwise have been by tracing many of Flora Annie Steel's books, and by generous loans.

My husband Anthony Powell and I shared two journeys through the sub-continent. I regard this book, which owes much to his criticism, as a token of gratitude for unfading Indian memories.

VIOLET POWELL

I

Miss Flora's Conceits

On New Year's Day, 1868, Flora Annie Steel began a life as new as the first day of the year. Twenty-four hours earlier she had become the bride of Henry William Steel. According to herself, preoccupation with dressing her bridesmaids had alone prevented her from bilking her own wedding. Her husband, on the other hand, declared that it was only the determination of his brother, the best man, that brought him to the altar. The bridegroom's career in the Indian Civil Service obliged the couple to sail almost immediately for the sub-continent, but this brave sink-or-swim plunge into the pool of matrimony brought a golden reward of unfailing devotion through-out half a century of adventure.

Flora Annie Webster had been born on April 2nd, 1847, at Sudbury Park, Harrow, then a country town, but now long over-run by the northward march of London. Eighty-two years later she opened her autobiography, *The Garden of Fidelity*, with a characteristically frank account of her own beginnings, and the effect she supposed them to have had on her own temperament. Her mother, Isabella MacCallum, heiress of a Jamaican plantation owner, had at the age of eighteen married a husband seventeen years older and had rapidly produced five children. A family row about money had caused Flora's father, George Webster, voluntarily to cease from marital relations, as his daughter put it. When these were resumed their first fruit was a sixth child and second daughter, Flora. Later in her career she pondered whether this abstinence on her father's part had not given her what she called an inborn dislike for the sensual side of life. The logic of this idea, with love and finance in opposition to each other, would seem to be somewhat confused, but whatever her personal distaste as a nove-list Flora never shirked the sexual implications of a situation.

1

This child of reconciliation joined a family that eventually numbered ten, the eleventh, an infant sister, having died. Flora saw the baby in her coffin, beautifully laid out, flowers in her hair and on her feet the new blue shoes she had worn at her first and last party. This sight gave the elder sister no feeling of dread, only a pang at having refused, the day before, to let the baby have a doll for which she had begged. Another little sister was born in later years, but the one who had died was never forgotten by Flora, which may be some excuse for the practice of letting a small child behold death as an actuality.

George Webster, the father of this tribe, was described almost with pride by his daughter as possessing the most violent temper of any man she had ever met. Having spent twenty years in India where the tempers of Europeans become notoriously eruptive, this judgement was backed by experience. Mrs Webster, on the other hand, seems to have struggled successfully against the storms brought about by her husband's light trigger temperament. Her principle with her children was to leave the room if they were rebellious. She never fought until she had chosen her ground and was sure of victory.

Mr Webster lacked this talent for strategy. Pursued by his father, one of Flora's brothers, aged five, fled to the nursery. Secure behind a locked door, the child shouted, "Give me an axe to kill Papa. Give me a gun to shoot Papa." Summoned to cope with what his father called "her" naughty child, his mother defused the situation in a calm sweet voice, remarking, "My dear! How did you come to put yourself in such a ridiculous position?"

When Flora was three years old, the cloud of bankruptcy broke over George Webster. His wife's large fortune, protected by ineffectual marriage settlements, was also swept away in the crash which involved the collapse of the Australasian Bank. The house in Palace Yard, which had been necessary for Mr Webster in his capacity as Scottish Parliamentary Agent, was given up and so was Sudbury Priory. The family crammed itself into a small house overlooking the cricket field of Harrow School, where the Webster sons were day boys. Their father took no particular interest in the education of his children, but their mother made up for his neglect by her dedicated and intelligent gauging of her family's needs. Not only did she see that they all learnt to read by the age of six but she attended to more wordly aspects. "My children may be rooks, but they shall never be pigeons," she said, teaching them the games of chance that might present opportunities to be one or the other.

Bankruptcy did not, apparently, affect the reputation of George

Webster, nor the social life of his children. The judge concerned in his case remarked that had Webster's advice been followed, the catastrophe would never have happened. On the social side the children were rich in playmates and parties. No-one seems to have attempted to discourage Flora's vanity about the golden hair which descended to the hem of her frocks. At one party she was stood on the centre piece of an ottoman, so that her bright mane could be properly admired by the company. She remembered this episode with complacency, but she had found no time to notice a nice little boy in his first Eton jacket who was to marry her in due course.

In the morning it was the custom for the children to visit their mother before she got up. Obviously needing to conserve her energies for the rigours of family life, Mrs Webster also sought spiritual comfort in a daily reading of Thomas à Kempis. With her natural turn for educating her brood, she turned this habit to profit by inciting her children to learn words rather than disconnected letters. If Mrs Webster included in her children's instruction the axiom of Thomas à Kempis "Whatsoever plans I devise for my own peace I know that my life cannot be without war and affliction," it was a lesson of which she herself must have known the value.

Encouraged to provide their own amusements, there were moments when the nursery children carried fertility of invention into dangerous displays. Luckily, soon after a visit to a circus, the nurse arrived in time to rescue the long-clothes baby from the arms of Flora, balanced as a bareback rider on the body of her next brother. The older brothers created a minor crisis every morning as they set out for "Bill", roll-call, at Harrow School. A succession of demands for their boots echoed down the stairs, the brother who was always late paradoxically asking for his in the gentlest manner.

The eldest son had passed on from Harrow to Haileybury, in preparation for going out to India as a Civilian, when news of the Indian Mutiny shook England with its horrors. As Flora's brother was due to leave for Madras in the following year, the Webster family took a particularly passionate view of the terrible events. Nana Sahib, believed to be the perfidious promoter of the massacre of Cawnpore, was executed in the form of a doll by the incensed little girl, who was to grow up to write novels remarkable for the breadth of their sympathy for both the Indian and the British point of view.

Before his bankruptcy, George Webster and his wife had entertained such friends as Thackeray and Cruikshank in their house in Palace Yard. If his temper was uncertain Mr Webster had also infinite resources of charm. This charm he knew how to use at home when it

3

suited his purposes, and, as he had a weakness for Flora, she benefited from the sunnier hours. Actually their father's misfortunes were moderated to the rest of the family by his increased reliance on his wife's encouragement, which had the effect of softening his violent moods. This was also, Flora thought, the happiest phase of her mother's life, for, though the first wave of children was growing up, there was still a supply of babies to be loved and petted.

These babies were baptised as Presbyterians, but when each grew old enough for church-going they joined the family procession to the parish church, where the Websters sat behind the vicarage pew. One of the brothers was in love with a daughter of the vicar, Mr Cunningham. Disregarding the gap of thirty years between their ages, he beguiled the tedium of the sermon by gazing at her. The prospective husband of another of the vicar's daughters found that even love could not make his future father-in-law's sermon tolerable. Becoming absorbed in playing balancing tricks with his umbrella, it was only when the pewful of Websters exploded into laughter that he realized that he had achieved the triumph of balancing his umbrella on his nose while seated in the vicarage pew.

After a period when his daily disgruntled departure for work in London had at least relieved some of the pressure on the cramped walls of the villa at Harrow, George Webster was given an appointment in Scotland. As Sheriff-Clerk of Forfarshire it was necessary for him to transport his family to the neighbourhood of his new post, which he was to hold until his death. A large house was found, only three miles from Forfar but isolated among woods and streams. The spaciousness was impressive after the congestion of the Harrow villa, but the move away from the school was an additional drain on even improved family finances. The Webster sons, previously day boys, now had to board and the fees for their keep had to be found. Beer, given to boarders when they had reached a certain standard of size and weight, may have been an extra expense, although Mrs Webster, with her firm grasp of essentials, had always given it to her sons at home when they could prove that they had grown and filled-out up to the level set for boarders.

The Webster caravan arrived at Forfar station at three in the morning, with trunks under tarpaulins lashed to the top of the coaches. George Webster, regarded in his time as a Liberal, even a Whig, in politics, had an attitude to what he saw as the proletariat that was autocratic, if benevolent. The railway staff ran to obey his shouted instructions rewarded by generous tips.

Less happy were the occasions when this stickler for perfection

4

chanced to see the infringement of a by-law relating to horse-drawn traffic. Regardless of the convenience of others, he would pursue offending carters with reproaches or even a summons. Yet, in spite of his intransigence his daughter Flora admired him. Somewhat strangely for a Radical conformist, he passed on to her a hatred of direct taxation, declaring that the incidence of exceptions in a tax is proof of its soundness or unsoundness. In later years Flora had an opportunity to demonstrate publicly against a tax she felt to be unjust.

At Burnside, the new home, there was more than enough room for the family, even when the boys were home for the holidays. There was no congestion when Isabella Webster added a seventh and final son to her total of eleven offspring. This child was born in 1858, so that nearly twenty years must have separated him from his eldest brother who, in that year, sailed for India. Flora missed her brothers intensely during the term time. The big house was quiet and empty, particularly when, her eldest sister having left the schoolroom, Flora found herself isolated between two age groups.

Mrs Webster behaved with characteristic decision. Explaining that, with the burden of so many sons at Harrow, to employ a governess for one daughter alone would be impracticable, she launched Flora on a scheme of self-education. Her daughter liked reading, playing the piano and sketching, for which she had shown promise. She was told to continue on these lines and she would find herself to be as well-educated as could be wished. Mrs Webster had judged her daughter's potentialities correctly. Except for six months at a school in Brussels, Flora from then on took charge of her own intellectual cultivation. There was no censorship of her reading, her mother saying that Flora would probably find "nasty" books dull. This theory, that her clean mind would be left unsullied, was proved by Flora's yawns as she struggled through *Tom Jones*.

In the great attic under the roof of Burnside, she read her way through a library of old-fashioned medical and philosophical works, which had been sent home by a doctor cousin in Jamaica, whence had also come the fortune so unhappily lost by George Webster. Exotic traces of this connection with Jamaica had still been apparent in the cramped villa at Harrow. In a tiny cupboard under the stairs a barrel of brown sugar had reposed, and from jars on its shelves greedy children could be given tastes of tamarinds and guava jelly. Once there had even been the excitement of seeing a live turtle, on the last lap of its journey to the soup tureen, kicking on the cupboard's floor.

After the move to Scotland, summer holidays were always spent with Mrs MacCallum, mother of Isabella Webster. This formidable grandmother lived in the West of Argyll, but she was also a repository of Jamaican lore, having gone to the island at the age of eighteen. Immediately she had married Mr MacCallum of Cousin's Cove. Isabella, also married at eighteen, was her only child. It was Mrs MacCallum's autocratic ways which had been a factor in the estrangement between Mr and Mrs Webster, eventually ended by the conception of Flora.

Although Mrs MacCallum was believed, in general, to take her son-in-law's advice, the family thought it unsafe to leave them alone together for fear of verbal warfare. The mother-in-law's attitude may, perhaps, have had some excuse, if it is remembered that Isabella's daughter's husband had contrived not only to give her eleven children but to lose the fortune that should have supported them. Besides her tales of Jamaica and of her Highland forebears, Mrs MacCallum, who died in 1872, had a rare claim to make for her grandfather. She had been born a Kennedy, of a father aged seventy-one in the year of her birth. He had himself been born to a father aged eighty-six, so Mrs MacCallum could boast that her grandfather had been twelve years old in 1649 when Charles I was beheaded. The Kennedys, Flora wrote, were a long-lived race. She might well have added that they must have also been an extremely potent one.

Summer holidays in the West Highlands were paradisaical. Mrs Webster even remained calm when a boatload of her children, aged from eight to eighteen, did not return home until midnight. It was unlucky that her grandmother did not live to see Flora's emergence as a novelist. Her granddaughter could only speculate if her books would have been treated with the ambivalence shown towards the yellow-backed novels that the Webster boys brought into the house, publications also known as "railway novels" and bought to beguile the long haul from Harrow to the West of Argyll. Pouncing on one of these before breakfast, the matriarch would remain immoveable in her leather armchair, meals passing unattended, until, in the afternoon, she would signal her return to reality by throwing the book across the room with the one word, "Trash".

Retreat to Scotland did not prevent visits to Harrow. A head-master of Harrow School had described Mrs Webster as a "real charmer", but among the next generation it was Flora who was admired by the music master for her voice. Objective about herself, Flora admitted that her voice was, indeed, a good mezzo-soprano, flexible enough to touch C. The music master persuaded her to sing to Joachim, the great violinist of that date. More practically, when Flora set out for India as a bride, it was this kind teacher who chose the pianoforte that was to share the adventures of camp and cantonment.

The link with Harrow also accounted for the continued acquaintance with the family of the nice little boy in his first Eton jacket, an unnoticed guest at the children's party where Flora had been set up to be admired as a golden-haired idol. The little boy's name was Henry William Steel, son of the Revd Thomas Steel, Housemaster of the Grove House, Harrow and Vicar of a parish with a particularly charming name, St Hippolyt's with Great Wymondly, Herts. It was, however, Mrs Thomas Steel, the Vicar's wife, who made the strongest impression on Flora, at a time when she did not know she was confronting a future mother-in-law. Beautiful and dominating, Mrs Thomas Steel summoned her son Henry, aged twenty-two to the breakfast table. When he continued to remain absorbed in the newspaper, his mother swept it from his hands with the statement that a child of any age should come when called.

When Flora met him again, Henry Steel was an undergraduate at Cambridge, presumably studying for entry into the Indian Civil Service. He passed the examination and sailed for India, returning on leave in 1867. In the meantime, Flora's eldest brother had returned from Madras on convalescent leave. Recovered, he became a kind of fairy godfather to the family, who had moved for three months to Edinburgh. According to Flora, now a "come out" young lady, some sort of revelry took the Websters out every night of the week.

From her self-education, Flora had collected much that was to be of value to her in the adventurous life she was to live. She had become a proficient needlewoman who would never have to rely on professional dressmakers. Her cooking was good enough for her to write a cookery book with confidence when that project came her way. With one of her sisters she had reared almost every kind of bird and animal except the delicate field-mouse, but such nursing of the furred and feathered had never prevented her from going out shooting with her brothers. Dressed in a spare pair of knickerbockers, she was mostly wanted to carry the game bag, though she struck at being burdened with more than two jack hares. More acrimony set in when she cried "Mark cock" and a brother brought down an owl. An argument as to who was to blame was settled by the owl himself digging his claws through Flora's thumb. Having become an active campaigner for the rights of women in her middle age, she found it comic to remember that, at the end of the day's sport, she had been in the habit of unlacing her brothers' shooting boots.

7

Although her influence was still strong in her family, Mrs Webster was beginning to suffer from the long years of strain and exertion. She could write plays for her children to act to an audience of servants, but she also suffered from headaches which prostrated her. It was then that she relied on the energy and efficiency of her daughter Flora to keep the wheels of the household turning. The brother Flora loved best had teased her about this energy, saying it would be an upas tree to shadow her life. Although she admitted that her childhood trick of crying, "I can do that", at the sight of any new handicraft had been a detestable habit, Flora herself after eight decades, believed that her decried energy had really been a blessing.

With a gift for painting that was so obvious that her father was urged to give her an artist's training, Flora also exercised her creativity in a way that was uniquely her own. Known to the household as "Miss Flora's Conceits" she was adept in an art form which mingled collage and peepshow. In a glazed box fairies with onion skin wings danced round a lake of mica in a landscape of moss. A halfpenny a peep was charged, and the few pennies raised were spent on materials for further productions. She also laid the foundation for a triumph of many years later by teaching herself the art of making animals from horse chestnuts. Dragons were a speciality, appropriate for someone who had a strong element of the dragon in her character.

It has been said that the Presbyterian Websters worshipped in the Church of England when at Harrow, but in Argyllshire religious arrangements were delightfully ecumenical. The local school house was used as meeting place for prayer by the Anglican curate, the Roman Catholic priest and the Calvinist minister on a system of rotation. As the school house doubled as the Post Office, all services included a game of General Post as one congregation succeeded another, a game used by Flora in her novel *Red Rowans*.

Like her brothers and sisters, baptised a Presbyterian, Flora alone of the family chose to be confirmed in the Church of England. Drawn to make this move by a feeling for High Church practices, her ardour was dampened by the impersonality of her preparation for Confirmation. Further doubts were implanted by a tract she happened to find in a railway carriage. Dealing with the efficacy of prayer, the tract told of a hungry tramp who knelt to pray for food, and immediately found some bread and meat wrapped in a handkerchief. Accepting this as an answer to prayer, the tramp ate gratefully what was obviously the dinner of some unfortunate workman. It would have been in the eighteen-sixties when Flora's faith was shaken by being asked to accept such absurdity, but the tract itself had been long popular with pious distributors. It was already a bane to clergymen in 1851 when Charlotte M. Yonge published *The Castle Builders*. The problem as to what the tramp did with the handkerchief being a matter for teasing the over-enthusiastic.

Flora was now twenty years old. Her family life was to her entirely sympathetic. Plays were acted which she produced. The house was full of visitors, food for the daily picnics being supplied by Flora's baking of veal pies and raspberry tarts. The family had a habit of declaring birthdays when they felt that life needed enlivening. For these, odes were written, for this was a generation who celebrated any event in verse with the ease of long practice.

Among the visitors of that summer of 1867 was Henry Steel and one of his brothers. Henry loved shooting and does not seem to have been disconcerted by the ebullient life lived by the Websters. According to Flora, Henry was a slim man, who, though he stood 5 ft 7 in height, never weighted more than eight stone. Flora herself was far from tall, her golden curls emphasizing the childishness of her round pink face. She had had more than one admirer who had written to propose marriage, but none of them had taken her fancy. Then there came a letter from Henry Steel, proposing not only marriage but a totally different life, far from the shadow of the Grampians. Faced with this momentous decision the spirit which moved her to cry, "I can do that!" at any new challenge must have helped to make up Flora's mind, for she accepted both a husband and the unknown Indian world where his career lay.

Looking back over the long happy years they had spent together, Flora still professed to be baffled as to why she and Henry had, in the words of the Prayer Book, consented together in Holy Matrimony. The emotion of being in love had, she thought, not been a factor, certainly not on her side. She could recollect no active courtship. Indeed she had been incensed at Henry making his proposal by letter rather than in person, not accepting his excuse that he was frightened of her. On Henry's side there was obviously more admiration than Flora quite liked to admit. If he felt that he would like the society and support of a wife among the lonely discomforts of isolated stations in the Punjab, he showed great perspicacity in choosing a girl who would not only be an efficient house mother but an intensely interested helper in his own work.

Flora's statement that she had never been in love is not entirely borne out by various episodes in her autobiography. If her interest in some of the remarkable men she met could not be called passion, she was obviously no stranger to strong, if platonic, admiration. In the meantime the fiancés' preparations for their new life together were essentially practical. Except for Flora's piano and the library of books that Henry's father insisted he should take with him, they asked for household goods as wedding presents. These were crated up and sent by the long sea route through the Bay of Biscay, the couple themselves travelling overland to Marseille. It has been mentioned already that a double attack of nerves had nearly stalled the wedding in its tracks. Additionally the last day of 1867 was bitterly cold and there seems to have been no-one except Flora with the presence of mind to revive a dying fire to warm the wedding guests.

Sailing for India was not entirely an expedition in a land of strangers for two of Flora's brothers were serving there as Civilians. Marriage, on the other hand, was a country about which she had a lack of information almost unbelievable today when sex education is illustrated by diagrams. Intelligent and well-read, Flora could still retain a basic ignorance of the processes of human reproduction that the birth of babies to a mother, a family of brothers and the rearing of assorted animals had been powerless to illuminate. *Tom Jones*, yawned over as boring, and the medical library sent home from Jamaica seem to have been equally unenlightening, leaving the girl of twenty to work out her own problems.

Flora's comments on her honeymoon, at once characteristic and self-revealing, may be quoted: ". . . many many women of my ignorantly-kept generation have told me that their honeymoon was spent in tears and fears. Mine was not. I simply stared. I accepted everything as a strange part of the Great Mystery of humanity and the world, though no child could have been more ignorant of natural happenings than I was . . . my distaste for realities was overborne by a desire to understand."

Whether or not Flora's "distaste for realities" was due, as she speculated that it might be, to sexual troubles between her parents, it is reassuring to find that, whatever strength of passion might be lacking, the sun shone on Flora's own married life. The Steels remained devoted to each other, sharing not only adventures but jokes. There was need for this sympathy in their wandering life, for the Indian Civil Service treated its junior members as something between expendable pawns and puppets on a string. Flora's parents must have had confidence in her adaptability, for they raised no objection, apparently, to their daughter leaving the nest on a flight to the infinite mystery of India. The nest itself may have been more peaceful when Flora, with her frenetic energy, her "conceits" and her bossiness, had sailed for the East, but it must also have been far duller.

10

II

Steel's Baby Bride

Although she was accustomed to the rough seas of the Western Approaches, Flora found the waves of the Bay of Bengal more thunderous than any met before. Even twenty years later Madras was still a notoriously difficult landing place, but in 1868 the process of coming ashore was positively archaic. Eleven years earlier J. B. East had painted the dramatic rush through the surf at the hands of naked boatmen from craft called *masulah*, cockleshells stitched together without nails. East's passengers were dressed in clothes that still echoed Regency fashions, but otherwise Flora's experience was identical.

Madras was not, as it happened, to be the scene of Flora's twenty year association with India, but so enthralled was she with the new sights and sounds that she almost forgot her joy at finding her eldest brother waiting to greet her. Of the two Webster boys already in India as Civilians, he was the one stationed in what was called "the benighted Presidency" of Madras. Anxious to initiate the bride into native gastronomic treats, her brother and the friends with whom he shared his chummery had telegraphed for a particularly fine specimen of mango. When it was cut open, they watched with pleasure as Flora dug out the first spoonful. It was also the last, for by some digestive quirk the pink and green flesh of the mango affected the bride as an emetic. Never one to like defeat, she tried again and again, but throughout her life in India the mango remained, to Flora, obstinately intolerable.

Journeying on through the Bay of Bengal, the young Steels arrived at Calcutta. Here they were greeted by Flora's brother George, now a Bengal Civilian. They had travelled without mishap to themselves, but the heavy luggage, sent by sea, had failed to keep

11

its rendezvous at Marseille, depriving Flora not only of her hot weather clothes but of her wedding dress. This was considered to be an essential garment when her brother presented her to his friends, so Flora cleverly manipulated white muslin and a white ribbon sash, a mock-up of the real thing which was wandering on the ocean. The effect was all too reminiscent of the nursery, so it was hardly surprising that, with her hair still in infantine curls, she should be labelled "Steel's baby bride".

It was the month of May, and the rains, which should have revived the country, had proved inadequate. Consequently, Flora had immediate experience of what Kipling called India's "hard service and poor payment". On the train to Delhi the thermometer stood at 117°, during a night in which the baby bride's skin became covered by a mass of blisters from mosquito bites. After her defeat by the mango, she scored a victory by unflinchingly drinking tea made with goat's milk, additionally horrible as the goats had browsed on the leaves of the castor oil plant. Having passed this test, she set herself to cross-question her host in Delhi on the myriad details which had caught her attention in the new Indian world. On his side her host, a policeman, was thought never to have recovered from the shock of his first sight of Mrs Henry Steel's round pink face under the golden curls still tied back with a bow in a childish manner.

At Delhi the railway ended. From then on the journey was by a carriage only to be described as a box on wheels. Bedding was spread on boards placed between the seats, from which bumpy resting place Flora had her first experience of the Grand Trunk Road. There are passages in the early chapters of *Kim* which wonderfully evoke the rich variety of life flowing through the great artery of Hind. In spite of the road's dust and monotonous flatness, Flora's own first impressions were touched with some of this same romance.

Her husband, habituated to Indian night travel was able to drop asleep, waking only at the square, stone caravanserai, set up by the Mughal Emperors for the shelter and refreshment of travellers. Here ponies, starveling creatures to the newcomer's eyes, were to be changed. If she found the road itself monotonous, Flora found this fluid panorama of camels, humped cattle and palm trees to be enthralling. Refusing to lie down, she sat with her feet thrust out of the window. Had she but known, this was the beginning of an absorption of Indian atmosphere which was to yield a rich harvest in her imagination.

It was by this means that the Steels reached Lahore, seat of the Punjab Government. Here Henry was to receive his orders as to

12

where his next station was to be. To find that the orders obliged them to travel back down the way they had come was an initiation for Flora. She faced for the first time the clumsiness of an administrative machine which could allow an officer of the ICS to trail round the sub-continent, when a letter to Bombay would have saved many miles by sea and land. Protest at such incompetence was frowned on, and likely to result in a black mark. New to such a situation, Flora held her tongue, probably for the last time throughout her husband's service as a Civilian. She soon decided that silence, in the face of error, is the greatest mistake that an honest man can make.

Stationed at Lahore was Henry Cunningham, son of the Vicar of Harrow, the scene being made even more homelike by the presence of his sister as housekeeper. She had been the first love of the brother who had prophesied that Flora's energy would shadow her life like an upas tree. Flora had called him her "next brother", as she had a reluctance to use the christian names of her immediate family. Admittedly she was in her eighties when she wrote her autobiography, but she carried her policy of not cluttering up her narrative with names to a bewildering extreme.

Among her omissions was that of the christian name of the husband with whom she had lived for nearly sixty years. Even her entry in the *Who's Who* of 1905 gave Henry Steel no more individuality than that of an 'Indian Civilian'. In *The Garden of Fidelity* her daughter Mabel remained equally anonymous. Flora's brothers' names can only be learnt indirectly, her sisters' not at all. This practice casts a rather unfair shadow on her own family, for she also omits the names of the crooked dealers, drunkards and adulterers who came her way. People she liked and admired were more frequently identified, but Flora left most of her family unmarked among the legion of bad hats.

At the Cunninghams' Flora first experienced what was called Punjab fever, an intermittent plague which was to follow her until her last day in India. After taking the bride into dinner, her host was smitten in the midst of the feast. Shaking, with tears running down his face, he barely held out until dessert had been reached. Malarial mosquitoes, as Flora put it, had not then been invented. Quinine was the only palliative for a fever which, in a matter of minutes, could reduce the sufferer to a delirious jelly. Fortunately, Henry Cunningham had the stamina to survive these attacks. He became a judge, a knight and the author of some frivolous novels of Anglo-Indian life. In this last field he was completely outclassed by Steel's Baby Bride.

13

Returning in the direction of Delhi, the Steels then took up their first posting at Ludhiana, not far from where Chandigarh, the modern, Le Corbusier-designed capital of the Punjab, now stands. The Deputy Commissioner's wife had taken her children to the hills, the other functionaries were unmarried. Consequently, when Flora collapsed, possibly as the result of seven months of new experiences in a strange climate, she was without the support of any European woman.

There are some indications that her collapse may have involved a miscarriage. For instance, Flora mentions that a sergeant's wife, fetched from the nearest cantonments, kept up a constant history of disaster, specializing in gruesome stories of young wives in her husband's regiment who had died at the birth of a first child. Henry Steel was out all day administering his district. As Flora lay perspiring in the phenomenal heat, she sympathised wryly with what her father's feelings must have been when her mother asked him how he had come to put himself in such a ridiculous position.

Summoning her sense of duty to stifle regrets for a less "hard service", Flora kept a grip of herself until rescue arrived by way of an invitation from Henry Steel's chief, Colonel Reynell Taylor, Commissioner of the Punjab. Transferred by *dhooli* to the hill station Kasauli, Flora, in a daze, could just realize that she was travelling through ravines glowing with wild dahlias. She was too ill to see her host for three weeks, but, when her convalescent eyes fell on what she called the preux chevalier of the Punjab, she thought him worthy of all earthly worship. Her determination that she had never been in love gave Flora licence, in her own eyes, to write with an enthusiasm which might normally be considered evidence of extreme sensibility. The tall figure, the curly fair hair speckled with grey and the candid blue eyes of Colonel Reynell Taylor set a standard for masculine grace which Flora thought to be still unmatched when she wrote of him sixty years later.

Recovered enough to wear her real wedding dress, Flora acted as hostess to Colonel Reynell Taylor. She teased away his reluctance, and persuaded him to tell how, on his charger Suleiman, he had defeated five mounted tribesmen among the rocks of the Khyber Pass. Not only did he set a standard of generous hospitality, but he left her with a moral precept that she strove ever after to practice. To the young bride's attempt at thanking him for his kindness, the Commissioner of the Punjab replied, "Pass it on, my dear, pass it on". Flora learnt later from Mrs Reynell Taylor that it was necessary

14

for her to intercept many of the appeals sent to her husband, in the interest of reserving funds for the education of his family.

At Ludhiana, the Steels now had a large new house, to be shared with the doctor of the station. Flora's piano, chosen for her with loving care by the music master at Harrow School, had finally caught up with its owner. The doctor happened to play the violin with skill, so the new house was filled with music and the laughter of congenial housemates. Laughter was needed when, after languishing for an unexplained period of months on the wharf at Karachi, two cases, one of linen, one of plate, were at last delivered.

The cases should have been filled with wedding presents, both pretty and practical, including the silver tea-pot which, together with an irreducible pension of £300 a year, was considered to be the status symbol of an Indian Civilian's wife or widow. Excited at the idea of seeing their new possessions the Steels opened the plate chest. Inside were five ivory-handled knives and the three glass stoppered bottles from a cruet stand, space being filled and weight made up by stones. Henry, Flora and their friend the doctor accepted the loss with shouts of laughter. Henceforth they made far better tea in a tea-pot of Rockingham china, tea superior to any that could have been brewed in the stolen silver status symbol.

At Ludhiana the ravine between the native town and the civil station did not serve as an isolating barrier. Drains ran into it even in the dry months, breeding the still unidentified malarial-bearing mosquitoes. Both Henry Steel and the doctor went down with what was still known as tertian ague, because the fever recurred regularly on the third day. To Hal, as the family called him, the strain was particularly severe on his light thin frame. There were, however, advantages in being such a lightweight, not only when it was a question of riding in races, at which he was expert.

It soon became necessary for Flora to be moved out of the burning plains before the birth of her child who was expected at Michaelmas. A house was taken for her at Kasauli, ninety miles from Ludhiana, but by laying out his ponies at well chosen points on the road her husband, riding light, was able to visit her from Friday to Sunday. On her own, Flora battled against the insects which crowded the house, attacking the centipedes with scissors. Even her calm was once shaken when, not looking up on being offered the tea-canister, she found she had dropped a scorpion into her tea cup.

By doses of quinine and health-giving spells in camp, Henry's fever had been no more than a recurrent nuisance until, two months before the baby's birth, his resistance collapsed. He was sent up to

Kasauli by the doctor in a state which would obviously preclude him from returning to the plains during the hot weather. Probably by yet another kind gesture from Reynell Taylor, the Steels were now offered the hill station of Dalhousie, on condition that they went there without delay. With Flora incapacitated by her pregnancy, her husband was obliged to make the move unassisted, among the goods to be packed being a library of books unusually valuable for a young Indian Civilian.

The Revd Thomas Steel, as has been mentioned, had insisted that this library should be taken out to India, perhaps from a schoolmasterly eagerness that his son should have books around him. On the way up to Dalhousie disaster overwhelmed the Steel library. Harrow prizes and books inherited from an uncle being pulped together in Indian river mud. Unfortunately, the ferry boat from which they were upset belonged to the Rajah of Karparthala. Government refused to press a claim for compensation, on the grounds that it would be politically inexpedient.

Flora's own journey, dusty miles behind jibbing ponies, ended in sudden enchantment. Transferred to a *dhooli*, she awoke to find that the bearers had set her down beside a fern-hung stream of Highland prettiness. Above her the sun was rising over what she learnt to call Holy Himalaya. This sight can catch the heart if seen from the air five hundred miles away. To a tired pregnant girl, lifting up her eyes from the foothills, it brought a revival of belief in life's bright promises. She was to need this spiritual comfort, for at Michaelmas came a cruel disappointment in the still-birth of a daughter.

Ill for three days beforehand, Flora found little comfort in the attention of an untrained nurse and the care of a doctor who was a stranger to her. The latter told her that, as she was young and likely to have other children, it had been thought better to save her and let the child take its chance. Flora was left with a haunted feeling, which came out often in her writing, that this loss might have been unnecessary. A feeling of mourning for her first born stayed with her ever afterwards, a grief for someone who had been part of herself but whom she was never to know.

She was shaken out of a convalescent watching of the mountain snows by the need for action. A crisis in her husband's office not only sent Flora bounding back into health, but gave her a first taste of blood in the world of Indian civil administration. As there had been apparently some misappropriation of funds, the newly appointed officer was ordered to send an immediate report and explanation. Henry Steel's transfer had been a break in the usual ICS routine of transfers and appointments, so he was faced with a bureaucratic machine halted at an unorthodox stopping place. Somewhat quaintly, Flora wrote that his attacks of fever and her illness having left Hal rather helpless, she undertook the business herself, the office clerks being in the ambiguous position of knowing too much.

If the loss of her child left a pain that time did not obliterate, work certainly braced her spirits. Digging among the files, Flora produced an exhaustive report. Government accepted her report, but Government was also revealed to her in all its convolutions, leaving her with a belief that efficiency might well depend on benevolent autocracy. The result of this crash course in administration left her with the well-grounded confidence that there was no aspect of bureaucracy which she could not tackle single-handed. This confidence was the foundation on which her career in India was to be built.

After the dust of the plains and the grim predictability of the tertian ague. Dalhousie seemed idyllic. Within two months of her disappointment, Flora was in the thick of the station's activities She organised a Christmas Eve Ball, produced a play at the New Year and the male choir sang to her accompaniment, for she also played the harmonium in the little church. Male singers were not, however, always prepared to accept Mrs Steel's musical criticism. When she hinted to a deep bass that he had sung a semi-breve rather than a minim, she got the setting-down reply that it sounded more solemn so sung. An answer that opens up attractive, if revolutionary, vistas of musical interpretation.

It was, as it happened, through her attempts at theatrical production that Flora made her first real contact with Indian life. As always in pursuit of perfection, she was determined to get what she wanted in the way of curtains, footlights and paints for the scenery. In her quest she broke through a barrier of language behind which so many of her English acquaintances remained in a sort of purdah of the intellect. An Indian bazaar, she found, could produce almost anything that was needful provided it was asked for by its right name. This could seldom be gleaned from the domestics in a household, because, with their employers, they moved in a limited vocabulary. Once Flora found how profitable it was to consult books and dictionaries, she moved swiftly on to studying the variations of language in whatever district she happened to find herself. Her scene painting also improved her sketching. She learned that hardest of art's lessons, the leaving out of inessentials.

Perched above the military convalescent station, the Steels clung to their hill-top throughout the winter. Views of uninhabited woods and towering mountains lay before them, but there were perils greater than the snowfalls on the steep paths. On the back of a very small pony, Flora was riding home in the dusk, when a leopard sprang from the bank above, cleared the pony's head and disappeared into the rhododendrons below. Flora was uncertain as to whether the leopard's intended prey had been her terrier trotting in front, or the pony itself. Scared off on this occasion, the leopard sneaked back later and took the legs off the Christmas turkey as it hung from the verandah roof.

Although when she was writing *The Garden of Fidelity* Flora frequently mentioned how glad she was to have kept so much of her zest into her eighty-third year, she was under no illusions as to her own mortality. It seems that she thought it wise to tell many of her stories to a finish, regardless of their chronology in her own life. As a writer she may not have wished to leave loose ends, should she find herself, as she wrote, "disappearing into thin air which is also the Lord's." Indeed this was the case before she completed the book.

An example of her method, sometimes confusing for her readers, may be found in her account of her friendship with Captain George White of the 92nd. Flora compresses their subsequent meetings into a few paragraphs, which hardly allow for her own development since the days in Dalhousie. White, a soldier in his thirties with a bleak professional future, was in charge of the men from his regiment sent up to convalesce in the hills. Gloomily, he would sit in the Steels' drawing room, talking of the unlikelihood that he would get his majority before the age of forty. Flora was only twenty-three, but she gave him the wise advice to do nothing until the last moment, although agreeing that it might be against his nature to be a soldier. White was adamant. He would be sending in his papers, indeed they were already on their way. Time was to show that he was as wrong in his estimation of his prospects as Flora was in her feeling that he might do better in some other career.

Having begun her sojourn at Dalhousie with the loss of a child, Flora concealed a second pregnancy from her family. This one had a happy ending in the birth of a daughter on December 10th 1870. A note with the one word *Peccavi* was scribbled to tell Mrs Webster of her first grandchild. When Sir Charles Napier had occupied Sind in 1844, *Punch* had celebrated his victory with a cartoon bearing the caption *Peccavi*. Flora may have felt that her mother was owed some apology for the kindly intended concealment. She wrote of the baby as "Sind", recalling that "Sind" had been "healthy, red, ugly". There is nothing to tell that the child's name was to be Mabel, but to her mother, who had so recently been called a "baby pride", the newcomer marked a milestone of achievement.

III

Flora Learns to Swim

Although Flora had persisted with her painting, and continued to
practise her singing, there is no evidence that she attempted to
publish any writings in the early years of her life in India. She did,
however, obviously possess that vital quality for a writer—a
tabulating memory, the gift of being able to lay a mental hand on
material when it is needed. The memory of the racecourse at
Dalhousie lay dormant, until Flora found she needed it for one of
the scenes of crooked racing for which she had a literary partiality.
Her baby's ayah, Fazli, had an even stronger influence on Flora's
future writing, although at the time she appeared only as a fascinating enigma to her employer.

Fazli was a hillwoman, neither Hindu nor Mahomedan, to which
latter faith most of Flora's servants were apt to belong. The ayah
was strikingly fair and handsome. Flora imagined that her past, a
mystery, must have been lurid; though she did not specify if the
luridness would have been due to Fazli's ancestry or to her own
adventures. Advances from the Mahomedan servants were
rebuffed by the beautiful, mysterious ayah. They then refused to
carry the nursery party in the *memsahib's dandi* (a chair carried by
bearers). The bearers, already scorned by Fazli, were then humiliated by Flora. She walked along the Mall at Dalhousie, while the
bearers were obliged to carry a load of stones in the *dandi*. No more
objections to taking out the ayah and the baby were heard, the load
of stones having been less painful than the general ridicule.

When Mabel was six months old, Flora was obliged to leave her
at the house of a friend. Although taking some pride in her com-
posure, on this occasion Flora showed enough emotion for the ayah
to remark on it. "You leave her in God's care, *memsahib*," said Fazli

This seemed to Flora to be both a message to trust in the goodness of God, and a rebuke to the Christian missionary view of the Indians as heathens.

Not only was Fazli a woman of spiritual stature, but as a nurse she was a paragon. Like Flora, seldom discomposed, the ayah was shocked on one occasion when the Steel family visited a village where a *memsahib* had never before been seen. Generally the baby was the centre of attention on such visits, but on that particular day Flora happened to be wearing scarlet stockings. The outraged Fazli's nurseling was neglected while the women of the village crowded round Flora, admiring her stockings and speculating as to whether she was the same brilliant colour all the way up.

This was in the early days of the Steels' posting at Kasur, which, like Lahore thirty-five miles away, now lies in Pakistan. At the beginning of their stay there was no doctor, no policeman, not even a European missionary. The isolation must have been a factor in arousing Flora's interest in the language spoken by the villagers, leading her to wish to understand the pattern of their lives. Henry Steel believed in keeping on the move through his district, spending much of the cold weather in camp. Shooting over the country gave him a knowledge deeper than that gained by accepting returns and passing them on, without personal experience of the problems involved. He once pointed this out to a superior, who, having complained of omissions in Steel's bureaucratic processes, was obliged to admit that shooting had made him impressively familiar with his district.

Although the happiest days for the Steels might be those they spent in camp, their house, which at Kasur was both office and residence, possessed a romantic charm far superior to the mundane bungalows in which many Indian Civilians sweated through the hot weather. Under a dome which had been built to house the tomb of a Mahomedan saint, Henry Steel administered justice, oaths being sworn on a testament that had belonged to his great grandfather, Mayor and Freeman of Berwick-on-Tweed. A flask of Ganges water was provided for those who preferred thus to sanctify their swearing. The dome was forty foot square, its five foot thick supporting walls making for coolness in the hot weather. The echoes made the process of justice additionally solemn, though Henry Steel was understandably discomposed by a note that he received one day from his clerk. It read, "Respected Gentleman—Am unable to attend court to-day. Wife run away with another man. Oh, Lord! How truly magnificent!"

21

Round the soaring dome, sitting rooms and bedrooms had been built, but they were insignificant attachments to a building in which it was possible to climb, by notches in the thick wall, to a platform where coolness could always be found. Temporarily vacating this portentous house, the Steels sailed for home leave in April 1871, the infant Mabel having been so well trained by Fazli that Flora felt no need to take an ayah with her on the voyage. To have done so would have been an expensive inconvenience, for whatever the charms of their leave, the parents must have known that it could only end in separation from their child.

Whether the risk to health was considered too great, or whether the feeling was inescapably strong that moral enervation would inevitably attend consistent spoiling by Indian servants, at that date few Europeans contemplated any other course. "The voices of their children are not heard within their homes," was the poignant summing-up of the situation by Lord Dufferin, a former Viceroy, when speaking at a Mansion House banquet on the sacrifices endemic in the ICS.

Flora's grandmother, Mrs MacCallum born Kennedy, had died in the winter before the Steels came on leave, so Mabel could not boast that she had seen a great-grandmother whose own grandfather had, as mentioned earlier, the remarkably distant birth date of 1637. Home leave seems to have coincided with yet another disappointment about a baby, but Flora, as before, was enigmatic on the subject. She only referred to her need for medical attention, later mentioning that the prospect of another child had become unlikely. She left her daughter asleep in her cot, and set off for Kasur with the prospect of home within which no child's voice would be heard.

The wells of Kasur were impregnated with borate of soda, inimical to almost all vegetation, but Henry Steel was determined that he would plant a garden wherever he happened to be, and however unpropitious the circumstances. On arriving at Kasur he had applied for a cut to be made from a canal that lay between his station and Lahore. Returning from leave he found that this had been done. According to his wife his green fingers then turned the dusty compound into an Eden of flowers and fruit. Additionally, a swimming bath, built by a long dead nabob, was filled. Flora declared that, like all West Highlanders, she had never learnt to swim, but whether this generalization was true or not her ignorance was soon corrected by her husband tipping her unexpectedly into the bath. He told her to swim to the end which she did, becoming proficient so quickly that in a week she was diving for hairpins from the bottom of the

22

bath. However irritating Flora's habit of crying, "I can do that!" might be, it undeniably stood her in good stead.

Henry Steel's swimming lesson was not typical of his usual kindly behaviour towards his wife, though he could act fast in an emergency, as when the eyes of a wild cat were seen glittering in the drain of the swimming pool. His naked rush for his gun was re-inforced by the fox terrier, who fell on the enemy feline, rolling it into a gutter. Apart from his shooting and riding, Hal was unreservedly happy among his dogs, chickens and ducks, with the garden that flourished under his green fingers as a background for his pets. Flora's problem, common to European women in India, was that of filling the empty days in a childless home. Its solution was one for which she had unconsciously prepared in the days when she had sat in the attic at Burnside, and read her way through a library of medical books, relics of that remote doctor cousin in Jamaica.

Medicine as a career was still, at that date, considered to brush off the bloom of refined womanhood. Apprehension of indelicacy was mingled with fear of the unknown. As the mother of a distinguished woman doctor of to-day remarked to her daughter, "Anything wrong with tubes is better not thought about." The term "tubes" would presumably have included the whole of the human digestive system, a secret under-the-skin railway into whose workings it was better not to pry.

Such a shrinking attitude was far from being Flora's. Armed with self-confidence, she had brought out to India a medicine chest equipped by the knowledge she had gained from studies in the attic of her old home. It was a medicine chest filled more ambitiously than by what Flora called "the amateur's pharmacopoeia" of grey powder, castor oil and ipecacuanha, to bind, to purge, and to make vomit, being the basic necessities of home treatment in the late nineteenth century. Flora's own medical education had been recognised as reasonably adequate by her dear friend the doctor at Ludhiana. He, rather drastically from a nursing point of view, had once dumped what she called "half a library" on her bed, telling her with a laugh that she knew as well as he did what was the matter.

When Mrs Steel, wife of the head of the district, began her doctoring of the women and children of Kasur, she had need of all her self-confidence. Immediately she was confronted by the only surviving wife of a Mahomedan gentleman. His previous wives had died, and this young girl was suffering acutely from puerperal fever. No woman would have consulted the native doctor who ran the dispensary, for Kasur having been originally a Pathan settlement,

23

purdah was strictly kept. The old wives' practice was to cage the patient, well wrapped-up, in an airless closet, on a fever-inducing diet of ginger, honey, and almonds. Sweeping aside protests, Flora moved the girl onto the roof, applying warmth to her feet, coolness to her head, and lime juice to her lips. Under God's care, the result was recovery. After which, Flora wrote, had she directed that a patient should be painted pea-green, she would have been obeyed.

Naturally, Flora was not always lucky with her cases, the customs of the country giving rise to situations which no skill could have alleviated. When she had widened her scope to include local education, she found one day that a boy of thirteen was too upset to learn a simple lesson. His explanation, given with tears, was that his baby was dying. His wife was twelve years old, the child a doomed first-born of immature parents. Flora learnt that such children were known among the women as "forerunners", hardly themselves expected to live, but messengers to signify that others would follow with a stronger chance of surviving.

On a more cheerful note, one husband, who thought of Flora as having brought his young wife back from death, insisted that he must express his gratitude with a present. Presents, as Flora learnt later in her career, were a matter of delicacy, sometimes leading to sinister accusations of bribery, or even to blackmail. Finally she compromised for a pair of gloves, her size being six. A pair that turned out to be size nine was proudly fetched from Lahore, but Flora's clever fingers manipulated the gloves into a semblance of a perfect fit.

The health of the Steels themselves stood up well to the climate of Kasur in the hot weather, though Hal's needed constant vigilance. Arsenic had not, at that date, quite such a lethal reputation as in modern times, but some surprise may be felt at the nonchalance with which Flora mentions that a doctor recommended it instead of quinine to keep her husband's fever at bay. Her own worst experience came from rashly summoning the native hospital assistant to extract a troublesome wisdom tooth. His mistreatment was such that an English dentist later assured her that she had suffered the direst agony that a human being could undergo. Having spent a fortnight beating her head against the bed while Hal fed her with brandy and water, Flora agreed with him. Red hot knitting needles eventually effected an end to the torture, in what sounds like a form of acupuncture. Unfortunately there is no mention of this interesting treatment in the medical notes of the household compendium of which Flora was subsequently co-author. It would have been less destructive than the recommendation of "remorseless' cauterization for dog bites, or amputation if a snake bite was known to be from a death-dealing species, though both were doubtless essential in the circumstances.

If, as Flora wrote later, the separation from her child was itself a wound that time did not cauterize, she did have some consolation in a pair of pets acquired by chance. One day, at Kasur, a squirrel's nest fell from the roof onto the dining room table. Its occupants, two minute blobs of pink jelly, presented Flora with the kind of challenge she had enjoyed in her Scottish girlhood. In a basket, warmed by a piece of hot brick to simulate the climate of their nest, she reared the infant squirrels, feeding them through a sparrow's feather nipple fixed to a scent bottle.

Tweedledum and Tweedledee, by name and appearance, grew up to be enchanting companions, pretty as only the chosen pets of Ram can be. The origin of their beautiful colour scheme, black stripes along golden brown backs, can be found in the *Ramayana*. This tells that the squirrel was the first animal to answer Ram's call for help in the search for his wife Sita, cruelly snatched from him by the demon Ravana. Drawing his fingers along the golden brown squirrel's back, Ram bade it live as a symbol of unclouded joy, only the black streaks of the god's fingers remaining as a mark of the cares of life.

The idea that divinely bestowed characteristics may become hereditary occurs frequently in religious mythology. For example, centuries after the days of Ram and his squirrel, the legend grew that the robin gained his red breast from Christ's blood, when the little bird had tried to drag out the nails at the crucifixion. With the marks of the god's fingers on their backs, Flora's squirrels carried out Ram's instruction to be symbols of unclouded joy. They travelled to England with her in collapsible cages. They even set themselves up as literary critics, sitting on the ink pot when they thought she was neglecting them for her writing. Like all fascinating pets, they effected many introductions for their owner, including one to an old Brahmin. He knew, he told Flora, that the *mem* must be a servant of Ram, because she was so good to Ram's own pets.

Looking back on the past, it seemed to Flora that she had, on the whole found Hindus less easy to get on with than Muslims. Possibly she was influenced by her earliest Indian experiences at Kasur, its townspeople being descended from the followers of sixteenth century Mughal invaders. It was among these heirs of conquerors that she first developed her gifts for doctoring and teaching. Here also she learnt the ways of the people of the river lands, which were to be the inspiration of her literary beginnings.

The Sutlej River had always a violent influence on lives and property in Henry Steel's district, but it was on the Beas, a northern tributary, that an invasion far earlier than any Mughal inroad had come to a halt. On the banks of the River Beas Alexander the Great's army had mutinously refused to advance further. Here, in 326 B.C., the Conqueror of the World—the Jullunder Sahib—had raised twelve altars to mark the easternmost point of his Indian invasion. Then he retreated along the path that was to lead him to his death in Babylon.

The twelve altars, objects of veneration to successive Indian kings, were at length swept away by the ever-changing course of the river. They did, however, last longer than the town which Alexander had commanded to be built in honour of that most famous of horses Bucephalus. Falling as rapidly as it had risen, this monument to hippophilia was already obliterated when Alexander passed by on his retreat. Twenty centuries had not modified the capricious habits of the rivers of the Punjab, depositing fertile silt at one point only to erode the fields at another. When Henry Steel went under canvas for his annual inspections, these watery advances and retreats were the cause of problems which he was expected to solve without fear or favour. To Flora they supplied much of the material that was to turn her into a writer.

Pots were set to sail down the Sutlej, as they must have been long before the days of Alexander. The direction in which they floated, by immemorial custom, decided which was to be the main stream, the accepted boundary between new fields of productive soil brought down by the river. A village would triumph if its pots to survive the test numbered more than those of a neighbouring rival. At night, round the village well, Flora would listen to the tales passed down through the generations by word of mouth, with an accuracy of memory that is said not to survive education.

Soon she learnt that it was prudent to ged rid of the orderly. His red-coated presence, with its suggestion of authority, inhibited the free flow of narrative, particularly if the theme was the cattle raids of the past. Henry Steel seems to have been a somewhat stern judge of his wife's verses, but he approved of a tale of local cattle rustling when put into galloping ballad form by Flora. Descended from freemen of Berwick-on-Tweed, he may well have been familiar with similar exploits on the Borders. In any case *Shurfu the Zaildar* survived to be published in Flora's first collection of Indian stories, *From the Five Rivers*.

Shurfu the Zaildar is represented as telling of the brave days when he swam the river in flood, with fifty-three head of cattle that had been lifted from him by a rival thief. At ease after the day's inspection of the *zail* (district), Shurfu is prepared to accept a glass or two of brandy, excusing this defiance of the Law of the Prophet by arguing that the Prophet had been ignorant of brandy, and had not had to suffer the pains of old age. The story is given its piquancy not so much by dare-devil cattle-rustling, but more by Shurfu's comments on how things are run by the Raj.

A good crop of accredited malefactors, *budmashes*, has been brought in, but Shurfu could easily fix a few more if the collector-sahib's schedules look a trifle thin. Warmed by the brandy, he feels he has reason to be complacent over his obligingness to the constantly changing whims of a turnover of officials. Shurfu concludes triumphantly, "Not a village of mine owns a dung heap. My mares are all Government brand." Admittedly there is decadence. The cattle thieves of yesterday, swashbucklers of the river lands, have sunk to being the money-lenders of to-day, a sad end for the profits of their dashing trade. Comfort can only be taken from the fact that the Guzar-i-Shurfu is still sung in the countryside.

Flora may have romanticised Shurfu's good-humoured tolerance of the bewildering hobbies of a succession of sahibs, but it was by listening to such tales that she learnt to recognize the rhythm of village life. In the early morning she would watch the women set off in single file for their day's work in the fields, walking erect as only those who balance bundles on their heads can walk. Near Kasur, against the fields of mustard, they can still be seen making their way in immemorial fashion, their veils bright spots of colour set like jewels in the cloth of gold mustard fields. Marching between the women, the children appear like punctuation marks in a sentence of tall writing. It was the ancestors of these women and children that Flora was to know, to love and to teach.

IV

You Do Know Most Things

If Flora Annie Steel's right to an entry in the *Dictionary of National Biography* rests chiefly on the success of her novel of the Mutiny, it was her activities in the field of Indian education that first gave her the insight shown so remarkably in *On the Face of the Waters*. Henry Steel's duties at Kasur included the inspection of schools, in which the low standard of the English lessons shocked his wife who accompanied him on these tours. To improve the standard she instituted reading classes in the garden of the domed courthouse, which was how she learnt the sad story, already mentioned, of the thirteen-year-old father.

After class the boys were brought into the house itself, where Flora sang them the sentimental ballads of the period. Although the tunes were totally different in tone and structure from the patterns of Indian music, her pupils found them delightful. They were even moved to tears by such especial favourites as "Home they brought her warrior dead". Curiously enough, the drawing-room ballad lingered in India long after the end of the Raj. Only a few years ago a translation of Tennyson's *Maud* could be heard as background music at a party in the state capital of Hyderabad. Flora would hardly have approved of this performance as she had expressed herself strongly on the absurdity of translating Tennyson's *Lotus Eaters* into garbled Urdu.

Impressed by the success and popularity of Flora's teaching methods, the Chief Native Administrator suggested that a girls school might be started. Female education was a delicate matter in India, as it led, inevitably, to questions of emancipation, not always relished by those who might be supposed to benefit from a freer life. As the suggestion came from an official who was also President of

28

the Municipal Committee, it was supported locally. Had the scheme originated with Flora, suspicions ranging from religious subversion to the kidnapping of daughters might have easily sabotaged the project.

Although there were few Hindus in Kasur, the benevolent balance kept by the Sirkar in educational matters required that, in any officially recognized school, both Hindu and Muslim teachers should, for a stiff wage, propound their separate creeds. This being arranged, a first class of alphabet scholars was recruited from among the children of the bazaar. A top class was formed by a few girls from richer homes who were able to recite parts of the Koran by heart.

These prodigies had also learnt by heart what Flora called the dubious tales of the first Persian primer, creating a false impression of reading aloud. The tale Flora quoted as an example of dubiousness concerned a man brought before a judge on the charge of stealing his neighbour's male donkey. The accused countered by showing that the only donkey he owned was indisputably female. The neighbour then remarked that the stolen donkey had not, after all, been "a very male one". Although Flora found it necessary to accept that sexuality supplied the only incident and excitement in the lives of many, if not most, Indian women, she objected to a reading primer that concentrated on the sexual attributes of donkeys, even if the lessons were learnt by ear rather than by eye.

Flora's influence with the schools was, of course, backed by the strength of her husband's position as Administrator and ex-officio President of the Municipal Council of Kasur. Every Sunday the Council was invited to a social meeting in the court-house garden, a creation of the hands of their President. On these occasions it was Flora's responsibility to see that the refreshments provided did not outrage any of the dietary principles of religion. Melons were abundant at Kasur, so that the ice delivered daily to the Steels from Lahore caused iced melon, a cooling and religiously unobjectionable offering, to be readily available.

At Christmas, more ambitiously, the Municipal Council were entertained to a Christmas dinner. Flora was careful that mutton, rather than beef, should be served, the pudding itself being innocent of suet and brandy. Such was the success of the pudding that in future Flora served it cold at her Sunday receptions, to follow the iced water melon. An outbreak of cholera made a precautionary change to a blander menu seem advisable, but the substitution of jelly and sponge cake was a failure. So strong a protest was made against these unwholesomely rich innovations that Flora, although believing that

29

iced melon and plum pudding were no diet for cholera time, returned to her original bill of fare, no casualties being subsequently reported.

As it was necessary to keep a balance in the community, at Kasur there were two female schools of each religious persuasion. To these schools was given an order for a bed cover to be embroidered, a counterpane to be presented to the Prince of Wales. The eldest son of the Great Mother across the sea, who was soon to be proclaimed Empress, had come on a cold weather visit to India, and his camp was to be set up near Lahore.

No-one will be surprised to learn that Flora squashed attempts to pass off the work of dextrous Delhi embroiderers as coming from the schools of Kasur. She had not yet developed her interest in traditional native handicrafts, a subject in which she became expert. With increased knowledge grew disgust, both at the failure of her compatriots to appreciate the special beauty of the diaper embroidery known as *phulkari* work, and at the native exploitation of shoddy imitations. At the time of the Prince's visit she still leant towards Western techniques, but her design, based on the Prince of Wales' feathers, was effective when worked onto Persian satin, the main problem being to keep the white satin clean from the effluvia, which seemed to Flora to breathe discoloration.

To accommodate the Royal Visit, a camp was pitched by what Flora invariably referred to as "Government" without a definite article. This may have been the practice of her husband and his colleagues in the ICS, but Flora often used it to give vent to her personal feelings. To her the power that ruled her husband's climb up the ladder of promotion frequently showed itself to be a boneheaded bureaucracy, at its best laboriously well-meaning, at its worst malevolent. Throughout her husband's service in India, Government also remained, in her eyes, a parsimonious wicked fairy, frequently blind to the rudimentary interests of the Service. Flora considered that official displays of niggardliness did more than anything else to lower the prestige of British rule in India.

The great camps in the days of the Mughals often covered miles of countryside, but always in the centre hung a lantern, proclaiming that here was the Lamp of Justice. Flora thought this to have been symbolism of a higher order than the British flag flown from the middle of such a lesser camp as was set up for the visit of the Prince. On the other hand, in her opinion, the principle of the orderly pitching of this temporary city still owed much in its precision to the pattern laid down by the Mughals.

Vegetation to soften the aspect of the sandy plain was supplied by quick-growing barley and cut sprays of chrysanthemem already in bud. This assistance of nature, slightly reminiscent of the Potemkin villages that attended the progresses of Catherine the Great of Russia, nevertheless provided a pretty background for a grand ball. Here the Prince picked out Mrs Henry Steel, not for her bright cheeks and yellow hair, but because he saw her to be the only woman present who knew how a Scottish reel should really be danced. Queen Victoria had been an enthusiastic promoter of reels, so her son could speak with knowledge gained by footing it at the Balmoral Ghillies Ball.

Flora accepted the compliment as partly due to an hereditary talent. At seventy-five her father could go through the intricacies of an eightsome with a light foot that would not have caused a jelly to wobble. His daughter thought of him as the Dancing Faun. Her husband seems to have been more misanthropic, for his dislike of continual human contacts led him to pitch their tents away from the general lay-out of the camp. Government, unimpressed by this spirit of independence, still sent in a bill of ten rupees a day for lighting and sanitation, neither of which was available to the Steels, who immediately counter-attacked.

In fact the Steels were in a strong position, Flora's cherished piano having been lent to the camp and installed in the Prince's drawing-room. It was no entirely loyalty that had prompted the loan. Necessity had not yet driven Flora to learn how to tune the instrument herself, but she knew that the art was possessed by a bandmaster at neighbouring Mian Mir and that he would certainly be summoned to restore the piano's notes to a pitch fit for a prince's ears. The financial scuffle that ensued was finally resolved when Henry Steel sent in a bill for sixteen rupees a day, the going rate for piano hire. Flora's private war with authority had not yet reached its full potential, but she was beginning to flex her muscles.

Her character was also to be strengthened by a variety of crises. An unexpected call from a local rajah had precipitated one of the most testing of these. The caller had delayed the Steels from setting out in their dog-cart, the mare in the shafts becoming restive with standing. She slipped her headstall and bolted, with Henry Steel tugging at the useless reins. There was an almighty crash, and he was thrown out into a bed of chrysanthemums, which had just been planted. They broke the keen gardener's fall and appropriately saved his life. Meanwhile he was insensible. Flora had the body carried indoors, to a background of panic cries from the entire household that their master was certainly dead.

She was not yet twenty-five but she acted with more sense than the lady in the ballad whose warrior was borne home dead and who "nor breathed, nor uttered sigh". There was no European help nearer than Lahore, thirty-five miles away, so she had no option but to rely on her own diagnosis. She settled for concussion, but no broken bones, which turned out to be correct. When her husband recovered he had no recollection of how the accident had come about, nor, presumably, of his wife's presence of mind.

Looking back on the continual necessity for relying on her own judgement, Flora thought that she might have become too autocratic in the isolation of Kasur. She speculated that, had she lived on stations with a large European personnel, she might have followed the usual habits of her compatriot women, benevolent in supporting good causes, but initiating little of her own account. Both from her own self-portrait and from what is known of her character there is little to support this view. Wherever she happened to find herself Flora's activities were never circumscribed by convention, though it was only at Kasur that her scope came to include municipal architecture.

Perhaps inflated by a diet of melon and Christmas pudding, the self-importance of Kasur's Municipal Council had led it to the conclusion, endemic in public bodies, that offices worthy of its deliberations should be built. Mrs Steel was consulted, the Council rightly trusting that she would take the subtlety of rank and caste into consideration. Flora drew up a scheme which included a large hall for state occasions, carefully calculated to seat the various officials in correct order. Additionally, she designed a verandah where visitors could squat with due regard to the gradations of caste. The design was acclaimed, an arched apse in the hall being particularly appreciated.

Government, in the shape of the Department of Public Works, took a different view. Striking out the apse and the verandah, it offered instead a singularly inappropriate design in the form of a Swiss chalet. Flora's friends on the Council stood firm, arguing that her plan would cost far less than the one which the D.P.W. wished to impose. Flora herself made some attempt to stop the scheme, as the arch of the apse would have a sixteen foot span and she had never before drawn such plans. She was over-ruled, but consoled herself that the Taj Mahal at Agra, and the Red Fort at Delhi, must have been built by ancestors of the old architect at Kasur who was to supervise that carrying out of her design.

Almost immediately after its completion Flora's apse, and the building of which it was the pride, were tested by the full force of a natural calamity which both triumphantly withstood. At Kasur the annual rainfall was meagre. An average of thirteen inches a year made life precarious should even such a small gift from heaven be witheld. For nine months no rain at all had fallen, both the monsoon and the winter rains having failed. At last, in despair, the Municipal Council came to Flora's Sunday reception with the announcement that prayers to heaven were the only hope of a harvest on earth. It was requested that permission might be granted for twelve Hindu yogis and twelve Mahomedan fakirs to be set naked in the sun, without food or water, for twenty-four hours. Such an appeal to heaven, made from strictly equal sectarian representation, was known to be infallible.

When faced with a custom that she thought to be unreasonably superstitious, Flora usually did her best to deflate the idea by gently joking. On this occasion she suggested that, as the recipe was certain to succeed, it might be well to qualify the request by specifying the amount of rain required. After discussion, this idea was vetoed as a blasphemous attempt to limit God's wisdom. In which case, Flora asked, would it not be better to let God decide whether or not rain should fall?

The Municipal Council went home unconvinced. Throughout the hours of a particularly stewing Monday, Flora thought with compassion of the twenty-four holy men, inescapably at prayer under the pitiless sun. Early on Tuesday she was awakened by a drop of water on her nose. It was raining as it might have rained on Noah. Even the stone dome of the courthouse was dripping, while the sun-baked brick of the living quarters ran with water. The bearer proclaimed that the ducks were drowning, while horses had to be rescued and furniture covered with carpets. At six o'clock a messenger from the city of Kasur arrived, half swimming and carrying in a tin box in his turban a message from the highest native official. It expressed succintly the general feeling, "Farewell, this is not rain. This is the Flood of God."

Almost twice the annual rainfall had come down in eight hours. Nearly a third of the houses of Kasur had collapsed into the mud from which their bricks had come. Flora did not mention what became of the holy men whose petitions had been so spectacularly answered, but she recorded that the mercifully few casualties had included the bearer who fetched ice daily from Lahore, a sadly unfair fate. Only when the flood (which had cut the Steels off from Kasur), had subsided, was the Municipal Council able to meet once again in the courthouse garden. Flora was then astounded by the respectful but reproving attitude of its members. Convinced that she had known of the coming deluge, they reproached her for choosing to keep the information to herself. To them her advice to pray for rain in due moderation meant that she had sure knowledge that the heavens were about to open. No ill-will seems to have been felt, only an awed belief in the *mem-sahiba's* powers of looking into the future. So strong was this credence that six weeks later, on the rumour that Flora had had a dream, the fifteen thousand inhabitants of Kasur withdrew to higher ground and camped out for the night.

Although probably the greatest, this was not the only tribute to the magical powers of the *mem-sahiba*. At her dispensary a pathetic mother, saying that time might lack to dispense medicine, asked that Flora should write her own name on a piece of paper. This the mother proposed to administer as a pill to her sick baby, in the confidence that the illness would be kept at bay until Flora could attend to the child next morning.

Apart from her supposed rapport with the capricious controllers of men's destinies, Mrs Steel was also respected as an arbitrator. This confidence that she represented the Lamp of Justice was magnificently demonstrated by a delegation from the river lands. Their community was squeezed by a shortage of acres to cultivate, and its members had decided to uproot themselves. It was proposed to Flora that, if she would buy thirty thousand acres, newly open to cultivation by the making of the Chenab canal, the community would move there *en masse*, wives, children, live and dead stock. Five thousand acres should be reserved for Henry Steel, "the angelic one", to shoot over. A fine house would be built for the *memsahiba*, their Begum, who would have freedom to go to the hills whenever she wished. In return her tenants would promise never to go to law, but to bring all quarrels for the Begum to settle.

The temptation to set up a private kingdom, where the wilderness might be made to blossom, was increased by the idea that Flora's arbitration would cut out the legal process by which the intermediary pleaders could ruin those whose cases they were employed to support. Refusal was, however, made inevitable by the strain that India imposed on Henry Steel's health. Flora could only enjoy in imagination the thought of what a gadfly she would have been on the flank of Government, had she set up as a Begum.

She had already had the opportunity to be a gadfly when she campaigned against the oppression of the husbandman by the usurer. Unwisely, as she wrote, the editor of the local paper at

Lahore asked her to write leaders when he happened to be indisposed. Flora took the chance to propound a scheme which would protect the peasants from foreclosure by making it against the interests of the usurer to turn the workers off the land and so lose his share of the produce of their labour. Nearly twenty years later the laws were amended as she had proposed, but by that time Flora had put forward many other unpopular views which she felt she was qualified by experience to express.

Government's feelings about the irrepressible Mrs Steel became obvious at a banquet when she happened to be sitting opposite the Secretary of the Lieutenant Governor of the Punjab. Unprovokedly, he addressed her across the table with a challenge he did not expect she could answer. Although she did know most things, he said, he was now going to puzzle her. It was unfortunate for him that the puzzle which he offered was a sentence of Gaelic greeting. From her youth in the West Highlands, Flora was not only able to reply politely, but to point out that, for addressing a lady, the Secretary's grammar was incorrect.

V

The Blue Poppy

Besides leaving many characters in *The Garden of Fidelity* anonymous, Flora juggled indiscriminately with the chronology of her career in India. According to her much loved grandson Neil Webster, she was determined that a book about herself should not be overloaded with dates and the names of others. This is understandable, but a scarcity of dates in their correct sequence makes the endless moves required by the Service hard to follow. It is therefore simpler to bring together three separate visits to Kashmir, dealing with them in one chapter, rather than inserting them as they probably occurred.

The first visit was made in 1876, the two Steels travelling with two male friends. Although a natural autocrat, Flora had no objection to being pampered when she was the only woman in a holiday party. Her female rival was her Highland terrier Spech. The latter gave birth to five puppies during the journey. Their accommodation was arranged by Flora with more attention to the comfort of the canine family than to local prejudice. Impressed by the rank of the Premier Commissioner of the Punjab, who was one of the party, the Maharajah of Kashmir had sent his palanquin to transport the honourable lady. Flora admitted that had she then understood how averse to dogs most Indians are, she would not herself have ridden her Arab pony, while Spech and the puppies travelled in luxury under the domed roof of the Maharajah's gorgeous jhan-pan.

The fourth member of the party was the Superintendent of Vaccination. He owned a clever sheepdog called Lovat, who not only kept Flora's terriers in order, but, if a shepherd was driving too hard a bargain, could be sent to cut out the fattest sheep from a flock. This example of pure magic invariably brought the transaction to a swift and awestruck conclusion.

Approaching Srinagar, progress became ever more impressive, for the Maharajah sent a royal barge to convey the travellers. The forty rowers showed their variety of fancy strokes, heart-shaped paddles throwing up a feathery line of spray to mark the barge's wake. At Srinagar itself a magnificent spread of sweetmeats, fruit and a tribute of a thousand and ten silver rupees was laid before these honoured guests. The rupees, an offering unacceptable to an official, were returned by the Premier Commissioner with suitably modest politeness. In contrast with this lavishness, Flora found that the famous Kashmir shawls were made in miserable conditions by overworked men and boys, paid a quarter of the wages that her party gave their baggage coolies. She was even more harrowed by meeting, at a point of marvellous scenic beauty, two men with drawn swords leading a handcuffed prisoner. She was told that he had killed his mother, and his air of scowling exhaustion haunted her mind for days.

Another encounter was made happier by Flora's own initiative and understanding of the religious sensitivity around her. At a regular halting place for Hindu pilgrims, the Muslim servants of the Commissioner's party pitched its tents insolently near the area recognized as allocated to holy men. A suggestion of moving camp was made, but Flora preferred to tackle the matter on her own. Wrapping her skirt closely round her, she walked into the gathering of naked, ash-smeared devotees. When one brushed too near her, she set up the *noli me tangere* of the pollution cry, which caused her to be welcomed on equal terms for a philosophical discussion. A yogi who looked like King Victor Emmanuel of Italy assured a newcomer who joined the party that there was nothing of harm in this sympathetic *mem*. Pleasure at her reception did not, however, lead Flora toward greater respect for swamies and sunnyasies. The only one she began to admire during her time in India spoilt his reputation for spirituality by displaying an undue respect for worldly power. He insisted that Flora should read the laudatory notice which Kaiser William II, then Crown Prince William, had written in the holy man's visitors book.

Five years later, in 1881, the two Steels set out again for Kashmir, determined to reach the sacred cave of Amarnath, this shrine lying sixteen thousand stormy feet above sea-level. Bad weather had prevented the Steels from achieving the ascent on their earlier tour. In the flood at Kasur, Flora had splashed about in the wading trousers of her fisherman husband. Even more emancipated, she now cut her hair short and wore knickerbockers, as she had out shooting when she had carried the game bag for her brothers. She rode on a high native saddle, thinking with gratitude of the Mughal Emperors for their strong building of the roadside serai which sheltered the travellers at night.

Before she left Lahore, Flora's health had been uncertain with a threat of cholera. Typically of her elastic temperament, the attack had been cured by a chat with a doctor who had been among her dancing partners in Edinburgh. This cure of auld lang syne was not complete, for Flora suffered a relapse on the road. Her condition cannot have been made more cheerful by the pathetic sight of a wayside cross over the grave of a five-month-old baby, the child of young parents, the father being only a lieutenant. This time, doses of whisky and chicken broth drove away the sickness, leaving Flora in awed contemplation of her animal powers of recuperation.

The cook hired for the trip was more of a problem than the *mem-sahiba*. He was reputedly younger than Flora's regular cook, who had pleaded age as an excuse to avoid the rough journey. The substitute had a strong black beard and appeared to be an agile walker. The Steels had given him money with which to buy warm clothes, but doubts as to his age and sense, started by the grey hairs sprouting through the dye of his beard, increased when, at the top of a snow-filled pass, he was seen to be in his usual white clothing, naturally almost stunned with cold. Flora wrapped him in a tartan rug, which ultimately saved the cook's life. He later took a short cut, disappeared, and was only just rescued alive when one of the search party saw the MacCallum tartan distinct against the snow.

Much of Flora's diary was a paean to the beauties of Kashmir's ravishing scenery. Here the flowers and fruit grew as they must have grown in the Garden of Eden. Other feelings were aroused when, at last, the sacred grotto of Amarnath was reached. At that date pilgrims made their last stage naked, and almost invariably drugged with Indian hemp. Hundreds consequently died on the way to this search for salvation. Arrived at the grotto, Flora found it to be almost commonplace, with a frozen spring at the back approximating in shape to the *lingam*, the phallic object of worship of the Saivis. There were no pilgrims struggling to achieve holiness as it was not the season, but Flora thought the grotto impressive from the sheer triviality of what it offered. The skeletons she had seen by the wayside had fallen seeking salvation, rather than a temple made with hands.

On the struggle back to relative civilization, Flora may have felt that she too was threatened with a pilgrim's death. After an ice-slide on a blanket down a precipice, she had to halt the coolies who were carrying her across a stream, her weight not being great enough to steady them against the current. Two more men were fetched to make a heavier team. It was then that Flora was told the delightful legend that bears, before fording a strongly running stream, habitually pick up a boulder to give themselves ballast. Believing from her own observation that any animal would be quite capable of making such a practical deduction, Flora, from her octogenarian pinnacle, defied her readers to doubt this example of ursine brilliance.

Although she undeniably enjoyed a good tussle with authority, Flora held firmly to the idea that she did not often lose her temper, at least not thoroughly. Whether others would have agreed with her estimate of her own calmness is debatable, but when the storm did break its thunder was worthy of a daughter of George Webster. In Kashmir she let fly at least twice. Once when an official of the Maharajah's attempted to extract, with blows, a tax from the coolies which Mrs Steel had already paid. She spoke angrily then, but on the second occasion she found words inadequate to express her fury.

During her third visit to Kashmir, a mule, rejected by Henry Steel on account of a frightful gall on its withers, was found to be still with the convoy, and staggering under the heaviest load. Regarding sick animals, on two legs or four, as under her special protection, Flora soaked her handkerchief in saline and fixed it to the sore with a bandage.

The men of the party having gone out shooting, Flora went later to visit her patient. She found that, her careful bandaging having been removed, flies swarmed over the poor beast's wound. Unluckily for the mule man, Flora was still in her riding habit with her whip in her hand. Sending for the offender she beat him till she was out of breath. She was cheered on by the rest of the coolies, who thoroughly enjoyed their fellow's obvious belief that he had been seized by a female demon. The demon herself admitted that her loss of temper always coincided with an unladylike desire to hit out. It was remembered in her family that when two Steel nephews had misbehaved her cry was, "Let me get at them while I'm hot!" Whatever she may have done to her nephews only the most dedicated opponents of corporal punishment would call her attack on the brutal mule owner unjustified.

It was on this third visit to Kashmir that Flora found a perfectly blue poppy. This was the crowning exotic beauty among flowers of such variety that in one morning she pressed thirty-two different species into her diary. Too rare to be picked as a collector's specimen, she left the poppy to bloom in cerulean purity on the hillside. She remembered it as if its petals had been cut from the sky, and perpetuated the memory in her novel based on the life of the Great Mughal. This book,

A Prince of Dreamers, ends with a conceit of Akbar asleep on the hillside, under his head a tuft of the blue poppies of heavenly rest.

While still based on Kasur, Flora, as stated, had already begun her career as a promoter and manager of schools. In her efforts she was helped by what the writers Somerville and Ross called "the incommunicable gift of being talked to." In her autobiography Flora gave an example of learning to manipulate this gift, showing incidentally that she was in the habit of travelling unescorted, without apprehension of insult or injury.

One evening she arrived at Kasur's nearest, but far from near, railway station. The mail phaeton, which she had expected to find, was not waiting. Her choice then lay between a night on a *charpoy* outside the police station, and the hiring of a native *ekka*. Having on a previous occasion lain sleepless on a *charpoy* while pariah dogs bayed the moon, Flora decided in favour of the *ekka*. Fashioned without nails like the *masulah* at Madras, the *ekka* was held together by leather thongs tied round its bamboo structure. The two foot square platform had a canopy from which hung curtains, always drawn by women to protect their modesty. Flora wrote that to sit an *ekka* sedately required practice, likening the necessary action to that of rising in one's stirrups. She also claimed to have seen six females crammed into the two-foot square space. A believable sight, for Indian country people have a prejudice against waste of space in any form of transport, a prejudice only made stronger by the introduction of the motor car.

The night was fair. The bells jingled from the straps that held the shafts onto the yoke. An *ekka* had no bridle or headstall, the driver sitting on a shaft while urging on the pony. Avid for the delights of the moment, Flora sat with the curtains flung wide open. So splendidly did the moonlight shine on the ripe corn, that she spoke to the driver, a big, black bearded Mahomedan of the fine promise of the harvest. He made no reply to this, nor to three further comments, so that Flora began to wonder if he was afflicted by deafness. Then he halted the *ekka*, got down and drew the curtains. The mother, he said, would be more comfortable if she saw less. From his reproachful tone Flora realized that she had not behaved like an honest wife, in the Shakespearean use of the phrase. Now that his passenger was decently hidden by curtains the driver was prepared for conversation, telling her things that she would have been sorry not to have learnt.

It will be remembered that the gift of a thousand and ten silver rupees had been returned with all courtesy to the Maharajah of Kashmir, who had offered them to the Premier Commissioner of the Punjab. This was an example of the Indian conviction that all adminis-

40

trators should be placated, and with luck put under an obligation, by the presentation of rich gifts. The custom clashed with the stiff rules forbidding the acceptance of anything that could be interpreted as a bribe, rules which experience had convinced the administrators themselves to be essential for uncorrupt government. Consequently, when the time came for the Steels to be transferred from Kasur, the question as to whether Flora could accept a leaving present had to be referred to Government itself. As the local authorities so earnestly desired to make the gift, permission was graciously granted for the wife of the departing Deputy Commissioner to accept it.

Lack of mock modesty and indeed on occasion of ordinary modesty, had the great advantage of giving Flora objectivity. She was certainly right to say that she had done more for Kasur over the years than would have been done by the wives of most British officials, but honesty and generosity caused her to add that she had received in return more than she had given. This was to be demonstrated when she came to draw on the stores of knowledge and understanding which she had gathered.

The presentation was to be made in the Town Hall, itself a memorial to Flora. It had been built in defiance of the Department of Public Works, but in spite of her fears its solidity had brilliantly vindicated the ideas by which she had designed it. She sat with her husband, who does not seem to have cared for ceremonial occasions, in the centre of the apse that had withstood the Flood of God. She awaited, she wrote, she knew not what.

The brooch that was handed to her, large, circular and of mixed content, had something of the air of pantomime jewellery, but the explanation of its composition went straight to the heart of the *mem-sahiba*. Every pearl, every gem, she was told, had been taken from the necklaces and bangles which adorned the womenfolk of those who had organized the tribute. Pearls encircled the brooch. The inner ring was of table diamonds and splinters of rubies, the centre, like the throne of God, being an emerald, roughly set with a verse of the Koran.

An attempt to speak her thanks was too much, even for Flora who took pride in her self-possession. She burst into tears, together with the assembled company. Had Flora, as she wrote rather tartly, lived in less isolation than prevailed at Kasur she might well, as a result of a few desultory good works, have ended up with a decoration from Government. Perhaps because of her refusal to compromise when she saw officially unpalatable truths, she was never to receive an honour for her medical or education work. Kasur gave her a Star of India, created for herself alone, a unique offering of love. The small value of its component parts did not, sadly, prevent the brooch from eventually being stolen when its owner was in England, but the sentiment of the givers remained undimmed by time or loss.

VI

The Servants of the Raj

One of the pleasures of Flora's first year at Dalhousie had been the friendship of the disappointed soldier, Captain George White. He had developed Flora's natural aptitude for listening and giving advice. Ten years later their paths crossed again when it became clear that the advice of the young girl had been the soundest that could be wished. Far from having sent in his papers, White was now Military Secretary to the Viceroy, having been decorated for gallantry in the Afghan War. His welcome was of the warmest, but Flora felt that she had the right to remind him, teasingly, that but for her prescience he might well have been long since retired. They met at a ball, where White, gorgeous in staff uniform, begged Flora not to be rude. She, however, could not resist making her point by fingering the gold oak leaves on the Military Secretary's collars and cuffs, emblems of several upward steps on the professional ladder at the top of which he eventually arrived.

Another of her notable Indian acquaintances, was John Lockwood Kipling. They met when he was Keeper of Native Arts and Crafts at the Museum of Lahore, but about him she was surprisingly reticent, although he joined her in illustrating school primers. As the pictures in *Kim* and *The Jungle Books* show, Lockwood Kipling was a sensitive artist, both in execution and literary appreciation. In the preface to *Life's Handicap*, Lockwood Kipling's son Rudyard pays tribute to the latter quality, writing that a few of the stories, "but the very best", had been given him by his father. The son's vast reputation has overshadowed the father's talents, but these were shown at their most attractive in illustrations to a revised edition of Flora's first published work.

As a literary début, *Wide-Awake Stories* was unassumingly aimed at an audience of children. Consisting of the tales she had listened to beside the village fires, it was published in India, with notes by Captain R. C. Temple. The circumstances of its publication were later to have a propitious influence on Flora's career as a writer, giving her an introduction to the publisher who did most to promote her books.

Wide-Awake Stories was subsequently re-issued in England as *Tales of the Punjab*. Neither the title nor the much expanded notes pleased Flora. She also remained ominously silent about Lockwood Kipling's illustrations. Inevitably her writing was often compared with Rudyard Kipling's, a standard against which the veracity of her material was measured. Consequently she may have wished to avoid an additional association with the name of Kipling. Flora herself sketched ceaselessly, with considerable skill, but it is doubtful if she could have reached the level of J.L.K. in the decorative capital which ornaments the beginning of most of the *Tales of the Punjab*. He displayed an infinite variety of invention in his treatment of the letter "O", giving a new excitement to each hallowed "Once Upon a Time".

Apart from friends who eventually became distinguished, fifteen changes of station brought Flora a fine collection of acquaintances among the eccentric and even among the disreputable. The worst of the latter she met just before her second visit to Kashmir, when the Steels spent a few weeks in what Flora called the most sterile in every way of the Punjab stations. Sterile it may have been, but dry in one sense it was not, the Steels being the only sober Civilians in the place. Although she wished to forget the grisly tragedy of the other young married pair on the station, her developing novelist's eye retained the impression in all its squalor.

The couple had been brought together by the husband's stepmother. This witchlike schemer, hoping apparently for disinheritance or death, wished to put a barrier between a doting father and a dissolute son. To further this plan, she brought about the marriage of the drunken young man to another tippler, the daughter of an English country clergyman, whose tolerance of her habits, Flora was to discover, had already been exhausted. The wife, mother of a puny baby aged two months, developed delirium tremens, through which she was nursed by Flora. To reach the paradise of Kashmir was a healing of the spirit, but Flora stored the episode in her mental drawer, bringing it forth when she was at work on her masterpiece.

Although Flora speculated that had she been one of many British

44

wives on a large station she might have frittered her time away, when she actually found herself in cantonments her energy asserted itself. Not only did she organize amusements and educational projects, her finger was frequently in the emotional pies of others. Her childhood's cry, "I can do that" echoed again when she determindly straightened out the marital difficulties of her neighbours. She prided herself that her own feelings were not involved in these disputes, but it seems that at times she did not achieve total objectivity.

Kipling, a writer whom Flora, as will be seen, rarely mentioned, used words to the effect that Stalky, like other great commanders, did not choose to dwell on past reverses. In *The Garden of Fidelity*, Flora chose only to include examples of her adroit redeeming of situations which were threatening the happiness of more than the people immediately concerned. At times she descended from her somewhat Olympian attitude towards the vagaries of sexual attraction, attempting with friendly ridicule to defuse a situation, much as she had tried with the same weapon to avert the marathon prayers for rain at Kasur.

This method seems to have been more effective with her European friends, linked as it was with bursts of truth not so much unvarnished as stripped bare. Herself pink-cheeked, far from statuesque, Flora had a generous appreciation of women who looked like tall, pale lilies. One of her successes as a mediator concerned just such an elegant creature, a woman with a face like a Della Robbia virgin under a crown of bronze hair. The devoted husband, an engineer, had sought to please this *princesse lointaine* by building her a superlative bath, lined with plaster that simulated marble. The wife said it was cold, building up a hundred grievances on this disappointment. Both combatants frequently appealed to Flora, who restrained her laughter sufficiently to suggest that the engineer might invent a furnace, or that the cold-blooded lady should bathe in a robe of blankets. Impervious to such commonplace suggestions, the wife threw her wedding ring to the floor, only Flora's intervention preventing the husband from picking it up. Mrs Steel, appointed umpire in the dispute by both parties, then fired off a salvo of home truths so effectively that twenty-five years of domestic peace ensued.

This was merely an internal wrangle. On other occasions Flora's diplomacy was more fully stretched. While maintaining that plain truth has the most potency when love has driven out reason, she admitted that the truth-teller runs the risk of being slaughtered, at least metaphorically. Indeed there was an occasion when Flora was actually threatened with death by shooting, having interfered disinterestedly in a situation where she has little commitment.

The station concerned was not that of the Steels, but the behaviour of the Head of this other District had given rise to a huge scandal. Unable to cope with the repercussions, those stationed there had taken the extreme step of agreeing that a report on their superior's wild proceedings should be sent to Government. Flora did not know this distraught official, but she heard from others that he had suffered a nervous breakdown in which he had indulged in some indiscriminate shooting. Aware that he had dependents, a wife and nine children at home, Flora moved undauntedly into action. She also moved into the official residence, where the infatuated man had installed what Mrs Steel described as a Becky Sharp.

For three days Flora attempted to steer the distressed lover into calmer water. She was hindered on the first two days by the adroit manoeuvres of the character she had christened Becky Sharp. Flora's strategy was also imperilled by threats from the Head of the District to shoot her, the would-be destroyer of his love idyll. Time, as will be seen, was inexorably running out, but on the third day the siren agreed to retire to a bungalow that had been prepared for her. The preparations must have been both rapid and necessary, for she gave birth to a child twenty-four hours later.

The immediate scandal, the wrecking of a career, having been averted, everyone sighed with relief. It was thought better, in the improved circumstances, not to draw to Government's attention the Head of the District's peccadillo. Flora was convinced, from this experience, that, offered an easy exit from an awkward situation, many people would gladly sacrifice passion to the social conventions. It seems that she acted on this principle on more than one occasion, for she mentions receiving letters of thanks from those who had been enabled, by her advice, to avoid a public dénouement.

There was another crisis, however, when more than advice was needed. In this instance Flora took physical steps to defuse a situation where passions had reached their flashpoint. There was also an element of comic opera in the plot of the triangular drama. The heroine was once again tall and svelte, pale-eyed and golden-haired, her beauty rendered more ethereal by clinging white draperies and a boa of white feathers. Her husband was good and kind, but essentially unromantic in his physical squatness. At their marriage, the husband had accepted that his very young wife was not in love with him. For her part she had promised to tell him if she did fall in love with anyone else. Almost inevitably this did happen, and it was then that Flora was appealed to for counsel and arbitration.

Her summing-up of the situation of the husband was bracing but practical. His rival, she did not hesitate to point out, was young, handsome, dashing, far more suitable as a pair to his wife than he could ever be. He must, Flora said, rely on mental strategy. On this principle he made the magnanimous suggestion that, trusting to the sense of honour of the parties concerned, letters might be exchanged for a year. After which he would be prepared to provide grounds on which his wife could divorce him. Incidentally, by the laws of the period, this would have been ranked as collusion, making divorce impossible had it come to the knowledge of the court. The agreement was made, but unhappily, if understandably, feelings were stronger than reasoned strategy. When the first letter arrived the husband brought it to his wife held in the tongs.

Flora's determination that she had never been in love has been mentioned earlier, but there is perhaps a tinge of wistfulness in her account of the steps which she took to disentangle this matrimonial imbroglio. Henry Steel had by now realized his wife's unstoppableness when setting to rights the affairs of her neighbours, Indian or European, but even he thought she was going too far when she deputised for her friend at a meeting with the all too attractive lover. Particularly did he look doubtful at the circumstances of the assignation, which was to take place in a deodar forest under a full moon.

Presumably the lover was disappointed when, instead of the elegant lady in her white draperies, rosy-cheeked Flora appeared, having left her *dandi* at a distance. The man Flora had come to meet was about her own age, at that time thirty-two, but in spite of Henry Steel's reasonable doubts as to the wisdom of the meeting it was sense rather than romance that was talked under those particular deodars. Convinced by Flora's argument that even an innocent assignation would be a falling away from the high standards by which the affair had been conducted, the lover escorted Flora back to her *dandi*. Whatever his hopes for the evening may have been, he concealed them. He kissed Flora's hand and made some high-minded remarks about ultimate truth, always regarded by Mrs Steel as a solution for human difficulties.

Ultimate truth, in this case, led the lover, his passion faded, to marry money. The wife, according to Flora, settled down to be a good woman, with a husband whose happiness had been saved by Flora's intervention. Not much given to self-criticism, she did, however, reflect that the situation might have been better resolved by less high-minded behaviour, though on the credit side no-one had been made unhappy for life.

Contemplating the upheavals that had threatened so many marriages during her years in India, Flora spoke up for friendship as opposed to passion. Defiantly she stated her belief that "perfect friendship, perfect love, can exist between a man and a woman to whom the thought of any physical tie is an abomination". Fortunately this somewhat bleak view of relations between men and women was modified when the educationalist was superseded by the novelist.

In the language of the ICS, Flora had now become the *burra mem*, the big lady, a position dictated by her husband's rise in seniority. Although she could make fun in her novels of bossy Englishwomen and their attempts at amateur theatricals, she was herself a keen producer of entertainments. These shows had often the additional purpose of distracting the minds of players and audience from the looming shadow of a cholera epidemic.

Posted to the large station of Sialkot, she added the task of playing the harmonium to her other undertakings. She was a friend of the padre's, but nevertheless enjoyed pulling his leg over the poor quality of his intoning. It would surely be better, she suggested, if he offered up the petition "Open thou our lips" before, rather than after, he attempted a note outside his range. Because she was female, the harmonium player was seated behind a pillar, even unable to see the choir for whom she played. Flora's sincere, if frivolous, suggestion, that she should conceal the shame of her feminine gender by cutting off her hair and wearing a surplice, was icily received by the clergyman, but there was something worse than a frivolous suggestion in store for the unhappy man.

For reasons unknown, the Maharajah of Kashmir had built a fine spire on the Anglican church. In this hung a peal of bells not customarily rung. On Easter day, however, the padre ordered that the bells should be rung to celebrate the great festival. Flowers had been arranged in profusion. Equally glowing were the soldiers in their scarlet coats, arms stacked at the end of the pews, as they had been ever since the Mutiny when worshippers had been taken by surprise.

When the bells rang in an unpractised jangle the sound rose above the voluntary "Lift up your heads", but then a sinister murmuration became audible. Swarms of wild bees had long been settled unmolested in the steeple. Now, disturbed by the unwonted peal, they descended onto the mass of flowers below, and onto the heads of the captive congregation. Flora thought it a deliciously funny contretemps when, defeated by this dive bombing attack, the General Officer Commanding was obliged to dismiss his agonized forces. The congregation, meanwhile, were striving frantically to brush the infuriated bees from each other's bonnets and hair.

Perhaps because she drew so much on her conversations with Indian servants when she was writing fiction, Flora did not tell many stories of them when she was writing her memoirs. The three characters she singled out for mention were widely contrasted, one coming from the essential but despised class of sweeper. Sweepers, Flora insisted, were likely to be the most active and virile, as well as the cleanest, of the domestics employed by the *sahib-logue*. Flushing lavatories did not then exist in India. Commodes had to be emptied with regularity by the sweeper, or the risk of disease vastly increased. It was one of these vital if lowly figures who was heard by Flora yelling for help. The brave sweeper had pinned a cobra to the ground with a spit from the kitchen, but not far enough from the tail to be out of reach of the flailing head. This snake died, as had its mate shortly before, when Flora, seeing a long brown rope dangling from the top of a door, caught the venomous intruder by slamming the door on its head.

Most tragic among the Steels' servants was an old gardener, skilled in his work, but crazed by his passion for his young wife and small son. He thought the latter could be encouraged to grow by being placed, like celery, under a glass cloche. Returning from home leave, Flora had the shock of hearing that this green-fingered patriarch had been hanged for killing his wife. She had crowned a campaign of torment by revealing that the adored child was not her husband's son. Flora, as her bearer stolidly told her the ill news, felt pity that, after such provocation, a life for a life should have been exacted from the devoted old man, who had grown asparagus to please her, and crawled on his hands and knees to thank her for treating him in illness.

Iman Khan, Flora's cook, has been mentioned earlier as one who felt too old to follow his adventurous young employers to Kashmir, deftly supplying them with an even older substitute. (It seems unreasonable for Flora to have grumbled that Iman Khan had slipped off to visit his own family, unseen for five years.) He was renowned as a chef, so much so that an aunt of Flora's had asked for his services when the Steels went on leave. The aunt was married to a most impressive general, had a kind nature and a good knowledge of the vernacular, so she seemed to be an excellent temporary employer for a favourite cook.

Flora thought that she had arranged matters, but on her return to India she found Iman Khan awaiting her. He had rebuffed the General's lady. He was willing to serve only district *sahibs*. He had served no other since the grim days of the Mutiny. Ricketts *sahib* had been killed in the bazaar on May 10th 1857, and he, faithful to his dead master's orders, had taken the widow and her children safely to the hills. It may have been this tale of faithfulness, which was often repeated, that implanted the idea of a novel of the Mutiny in the mind of Flora to whom Nana Sahib had been an ogre of the nursery.

Flora's final story concerning Iman Khan had a sad ending, gastronomically and even politically. She had taken to cattle-raising with the purpose of supplying milk to the large number of infants there happened to be in cantonments. Consequently she was in a position to fatten a prime beast for the Christmas season, when the Lieutenant-Governor's camp would be pitched in the district. It was Iman Khan who had suggested that the *burra mem's* beef might well be offered for sale to the camp, since it was superior to that for sale in the bazaar. Under Flora's supervision the beef was cut up into joints and sent to the camp. The cook's distress was intense when only the hump and the tongue were bought, the rest of the carcass being returned to the *burra mem* as too expensive.

The bulk of the meat would have gone as a Christmas dole to the clerks serving the Lieutenant Governor. They would now be presented with slightly cheaper but inferior joints bought in the bazaar. To Iman Khan such stinginess seemed to portend nothing less than the end of the Raj. He was only slightly cheered at the prospect of exercising his ingenuity on the many and varied joints that had been returned to his kitchen. However, even this hope was disappointed for, hospitable as the Steels undeniably were, the race against decay being lost, half the beast had to be buried.

An outbreak of cholera might make special demands on Flora's courage, both in minimizing the death toll among nervous women and organising entertainments to distract the attention of soldiers and civilians from the threat of a sudden, agonizing death. She was also well aware of another medical problem, recognizing that among the troops venereal disease was a sinister, ever present enemy. Kipling, writing of an identical period, wished that he could have had the opportunity to treat six hundred priests, who proclaimed that the wage of sin was death, as private soldiers were treated in the India of his youth.

The illogical attitude which banned both medical examination of the frequently diseased bazaar prostitutes, and the precautions which might have protected their soldier clients, resulted in hospitals filled with hundreds of incapacitated men. Flora remembered, as did Kipling, the atmosphere of hopeless depression, even among patients well enough to sit out on the verandahs. With a doctor friend she discussed the lack of rudimentary commonsense, which treated venereal disease as a moral lapse, but neglected inspections which might have checked the mischief.

Flora's novels show that she was by no means ignorant of the various categories of Indian courtesans, many of whom had such a deplorable effect on the health of the army. She even showed some admiration for those whose talents had raised them to the top of their profession. On the one occasion, however, when she was herself insulted by a bazaar prostitute she acted with uninhibited swiftness. Ignorant of the low character of the street through which she happened to be walking, she did not accept that such a blunder justified a lewd woman in throwing a "bad word" at her. With no attention to the probable illegality, Flora immediately hauled the offender before the local Indian magistrate for using language likely to cause a breach of the peace. If a fine was imposed, Flora does not say, but she was determined not to be known in any brothel quarter as a passer-by who would meekly accept insult.

It was during a cholera epidemic that Flora had her most spectacular success as a screen painter. In the circumstances she thought that a back drop of the White Cliffs of Old England might enliven spirits depressed by "the Lord of the Swarming Town", as Charles Kingsley called the cholera. The cliffs appeared evocatively good, but Flora was not satisfied by her attempt to create a wave throwing up spray, until she slipped on the ladder and upset the pot of whitewash. The sensational effect drew rounds of applause from the audience, an audience that invariably included a single gentleman, impeccably dressed from his white tie to the flower in his buttonhole. He always occupied the same seat in the second row of those which, for top price, could be booked in advance. His elegance at night contrasted with his daytime position as a bombadier in the artillery, his presumably gentle origins sunk in the life of the barracks. His background remained for ever among the unsolved mysteries Flora met with in India. Nothing more was known than could be deduced by his fashionable appearance when he applauded the spray breaking over the White Cliffs of Old England.

VII

Sunburnt Little Lady in a Wide Pith Hat

The first schools set up in Kasur were only the beginning of an educational build-up which brought not merely fame but danger to its promoter. A sudden dash home to Scotland, which failed in its object of seeing her mother before her death, resulted in an increase of family life. Flora returned to India bringing with her Daisy, her youngest sister, and Mabel, her daughter, now aged twelve. Daisy was only in her early thirties, but the year's visit did not result in her finding a husband in India, nor indeed anywhere else. Mabel, on the other hand, was in due course to have her own Indian experience as a married woman. In the meantime she returned home with her aunt, but her mother had some compensation for her child's departure in being offered a semi-official position in Education.

This offer was made while the Steels were still stationed in an outlying district, their postings alternating between the remote and the central, by whims of Government that Flora never entirely fathomed. Each transfer did, however, yield its special harvest to Flora's retentive mind. It was, for example, at one end of the Punjab that she stored away the legend of the mysterious Lal, which in after years was to be the key that opened to her the door of literary life.

On the other hand, down on the delta, at the confluence of the rivers Indus and Sutlej, Flora found that the strictly local dialect, a variety of Sindhi, made the setting up of female schools impracticable. As she struggled to master the strange twists of the language she was fascinated to find that the women spoke a dialect within a dialect, using a grammar peculiar to themselves. Compared with the aridity of Kasur, it was a fertile countryside. Rain may have seldom fallen, but the rivers watered the land from below, the children growing fat on the abundance that fell from the date palms.

Prevented by the complications of dialect from starting female schools, Flora, by now an almost compulsive educationalist, turned her attention to the wives of other officials on the station. These happened to be "country-bred", a term which carried an implication of Indian blood, whether applied to horses or humans. Stoutly British in their attitude of mind, the "home" they spoke of was to them an unvisited location. They listened complacently to Flora's readings aloud from Thackeray, Dickens and Scott, although these works can hardly have given them an up-to-date idea of conditions at "home". A more heady literary diet was also appreciated. Flora brushed up her French by translating at sight the novels of George Sand, an author whom Flora may have admired but with whom, in her attitude to life and love, she could have had little in common.

If the station on the delta had a burgeoning charm, there was fascination of a different kind when the Steels were moved to a post near the Chenab canal. Here the great Salt Hedge of cacti, planted as a natural barrier against salt smugglers, ramped across the country-side, a grey-green background for a myriad multi-coloured butter-flies. It was here also that Flora was struck by the superior physique of the farmers and their families. She credited this to the local system of cultivation, which required as many female hands as could be mustered. Consequently, while fathers followed the custom of bestowing their daughters in marriage before the age of puberty, they clung to the girls as long as they could for the benefit of their labour. Sometimes the husbands were even reduced to claiming their brides by legal action. When the delayed consummation took place the young wives were fully developed. Instead of little doomed "forerunners", Flora noted that these more mature mothers pro-duced children both stronger and healthier.

The Steels had not only themselves to consider when seeking a house convenient for Hal's work and Flora's new inspectorate. By now seasoned travellers, the squirrels had become part of the family. Houses around Lahore were almost impossible to find, but the Steels had vision. They were prepared to live in any house that they could make attractive, not limiting themselves to a feeble parody of an English home. They discovered that Government owned a garden, with a *Bara dari*, or garden house, in the middle of a grove of mango and orange trees.

The orange trees had been originally imported from Malta. They bore blood oranges of rare quality, sold for a high price, which Flora discovered had not been credited to Government, the owner of the grove. Typically, Flora rectified this delinquency when she moved

53

herself, her husband and the squirrels into the enchanting *Bara dari*. To make the house habitable it was only necessary to build a staircase to reach the upper room, where slender columns, standing on a tessellated pavement, supported a roof of looking-glass and gold. Outside four marble gullies were filled with pale pink Persian roses. According to the gardener, these magical rose bushes opened their buds at dawn with a faint sob of joy at the return of day. The squirrels found this to be an admirable home. They feasted on mango nectar, multiplied and brought wild friends to join in a scramble over their foster mother.

Presumably in consideration of his wife's appointment as Inspectress of Schools, Henry Steel had managed to get an agreement that he would not be moved except under necessity. It was administratively convenient, even for capricious authorities, that the Inspectress should be lodged near Lahore. Flora had some reason to hope that she would have a secure base from which to get to grips with her new kingdom. It was an imposing kingdom, covering fourteen thousand square miles. Peshawar, footstool of the Himalayas, was its north-western point, while to the south-east Delhi, not yet seat of the Government of India, was included.

Early in the course of her work, Flora found herself approached by what she called a comparatively high Indian official. To her surprise he offered her a beautiful sapphire ring, for which gift she could see no reason. Remembering that she now had something of an official position, she told her husband. Steel reprimanded the would-be giver, but accepted the excuse that the latter had previously made such a present without meeting with reproach. A promise never to do such a thing again was made, allowing Flora to put the episode from her mind. She had not found the official concerned attractive, but she was baffled as to his motive. Later, sinister developments were to reveal the purpose of the rejected bribe.

Flora's duties included the inspection of mission schools, with the power to recommend the amount which Government should allow for scholarship pupils. Although on good terms with the mission ladies who ran the schools, Flora wished to be very certain that the money allocated went towards the teaching of the pupils, without deduction for the work of the mission. She also disapproved of a tendency among the mission ladies to show too much abasement when in contact with the grander Indian ladies, such as members of the family of the last deposed Mughal Emperor of Delhi.

Confident in her own position, Flora took pains to be accepted as one who knew her way through the labyrinth of Indian etiquette.

Particularly when she was to visit a Nawabin of the former royal family did she assure herself of the correct ritual. The Nawabin held a purdah class at her house in Delhi, to which Flora was escorted by the mission ladies. It was a surprise to find the arched entrance crowded with rakish young men engaged in gambling and matching fighting quails. As no insulting remarks were made (Flora, as has been seen, reacted swiftly on such occasions) she was prepared to pass in without objection. She was not, on the other hand, prepared to accept a Nawabin who not only received her in a dirty dress, spitting *pan* unceremoniously, but summoned a woman of the sweeper class to read her lesson. Enraged by this mockery of herself and of education, Flora refused to speak directly to the Nawabin, briskly telling the mission lady that she was taking her leave. The Nawabin, Flora told her quaking missionary companion, was treating her visitor as she would not have dared to treat her youngest sister-in-law, an ultimate of bad manners.

Shock action had its effect. Half an hour later, Flora was received with the correct degree of ceremony, to which she responded correctly. Even the entrance hall had been cleared of its layabouts. Flora considered that she had based her behaviour on that of her hero John Nicholson. The youngest of three generals in an audience at the time of the Mutiny, he had refused to accept that native chiefs should appear with their shoes on, knowing that to do so without rebuke would be seen as a sign of weakening authority. His action was commemorated by *The Ballad of John Nicholson* with the stirring lines:

"Take off, take off those shoes of pride,
And bear them whence you came"

Flora's situation had lacked the peril which beset Nicholson, but she was equally determined to enforce respect. Recognizing defeat by a worthy opponent, the Nawabin even went so far as to send an unprecedented gift of fruit and flowers to the mission ladies. It is possible to get an idea of Flora as she saw herself in her rôle as Inspectress, from a novel in which she looked at the tangled question of an Indian's assimilation of an English education.

Voices in the Night, published in 1900 when Flora had said a last good-bye to India, deals with the agonizing predicament of a young Brahmin. Whatever the value of his studies in London, he has made the mistake of contracting an uncomfortable marriage with a somewhat shopworn English girl. Back in his native city, the goddess Kali regains a grip on his heart, if not his reason. The dual personality of Chris Davenant and Krishn Davenund struggles in civil war, while in the background the foundation ceremonies of an Anglo-Vernacular College illustrate Flora's opinion of the absurdity of trying to mix antipathetic cultures.

It is a garden party scene. The Secretary-to-Government stands somewhat back, as official good manners would dictate, while the presentation of diplomas, tokens of good will rather than of learning, takes place. The Secretary inquires of "a sunburnt little lady in a wide pith hat" if she belongs to this newly founded organization for promoting cultural friendship between the rulers and the ruled. His tone is rather patronizing, but the little lady, clearly a self-portrait of Flora, pulls no punches. "Who, I?" she answered cheerfully, "Oh dear, no—I am not often in at headquarters, and I get on all right with my schools and all that sort of thing without it, so it doesn't seem worthwhile."

Whether this was the Secretary-to-Government who had made the mistake of greeting her in Gaelic or merely a prototype, Flora made her opinion of official attitudes only too clear. She went on to write that while this "man of headquarters" calmly watched what was to the practical educationalist a futile ceremony, immemorial India was otherwise engaged. Two women might be seen sweeping up "a prize of horse droppings" on the perimeter of the assembly, a prize which would be dried and used as fuel to cook the evening chupatti.

Flora, by taking on her inspectorship, found that she was sailing in choppy seas where, to extend the metaphor, she was regarded as a particularly stormy petrel by the men of headquarters. Among her pupils, on the other hand, she became increasingly popular, although there was strong objection when she changed the system which awarded a prize to every child who attended. When reason failed to convince parents and pupils of the absurdity of such a lack of competition, Flora tried ridicule. To please the mothers, she said, in future the first prize would be given to the best scholar, the second to the worst, a topping and tailing principle to be followed throughout. By this nonsensical approach she made her point, afterwards soothing wounded pride by generous awards.

The pupils themselves were of all ages and many conditions. Six rupees as a scholarship grant was of considerable value to the majority of families, which accounted for such students as the sixteen-year-old girl, married to an illiterate husband, who suckled her first baby while she studied vulgar fractions. More enterprising was a child of ten, who bargained with Flora that she could be given sixpence for every scholar she presented able to say and write the alphabet, and also to cypher to one hundred. The child had realized that an inordinate amount of time and teaching was wasted on the alphabet class. Her brilliant plan was profitable to all concerned.

Additionally, there was the ancient bespectacled spinster who chaperoned the pupils through the moral and physical perils of the bazaar. She found her authority slipping because of her ignorance of arithmetic, about which the little horrors in her charge mocked her. Division, in fact, proved to be beyond her, but the simpler branches were mastered. In the interests of discipline, Flora found it advisable, on occasion, to give this venerable student full marks.

If Flora used some details from the great scandal which haunted her years as a school inspectress to give realism to *Voices in the Night*, the experience of the scandal itself would have dismayed anyone less pugnaciously sure of her own rightness. The University of the Punjab, a pet project of the then Governor, was not, it seemed, being conducted by the highest academic standards. Although good at talking, Flora had, as mentioned earlier, the gift of being talked to. More and more she found herself hearing unsavoury rumours of the means by which the incompetent bought themselves into Government service. The University was said to have supplied a diploma to a junior official in the Forest Department who could barely write. How could this have come about except by corruption?

When cautious hints that an inquiry would be desirable met with blank lack of interest, Flora tackled the senior Indian official of the Punjab, a man of great responsibility and corresponding integrity. Asked what he and his countrymen thought of the reputed scandal, his answer sent Flora off on the warpath. *Mir Sahib* told her that the British were considered to be aware of the scandal, but wished to ignore it for their own convenience. No one, Flora replied, should ever again dare, or have reason, to say such a thing to her.

According to her own account, Flora could, on occasion, restrain herself when she knew that official mistakes were being made. She did not wish it to seem, to quote an old fashioned expression, that the grey mare was the better horse. Rare might be a more appropriate word than occasional to describe those moments of self-control, when she strove to avoid prejudicing her husband's position in the Service. Certainly in the matter of the University scandal she advanced unhesitatingly, although she met an opposition both formidable in itself and unscrupulous in its methods. With the idea of removing the gadfly Mrs Steel from the scene of immediate action, Henry Steel was transferred to the other end of the Punjab. Unperturbed, his wife remained among the mangoes and oranges of the *Bari dari*, which for the moment spiked the guns of her enemies.

When Government was unwise enough to inquire why she had not followed her husband, Flora hit back with the unanswerable statement that she was not, as far as she knew, under the orders of Government as to where she should live. The letter of inquiry had been sent to Henry Steel, but he had passed it on to his wife to answer. The wretched Secretary-to-Government, who had presumably hoped to get rid of this thorn in his administrative pillow, asked in despair if Steel could not keep his wife in order. He got no comfort. Henry's suggestion was that he should take her for a month and try.

For a year Flora lived alone in the *Bara dari*, sleeping on the roof under the stars while her squirrels kept her company. Charges were trumped up against her, but she was protected to a certain extent by the authorities' recognition of the value of her work. Her pupils also knew its value, showing the appreciation from their hearts by their wish to protect her. Flora was told that her scholars, nearly four hundred in number, aged from four to fourteen, wished to set a watch on her behalf. To demonstrate their ability to do so, she was bidden to come down at daybreak to the big school. Here she would find the door barred, but she would hear singing voices within the building. The password was for her to sing, "Little birds, little birds, why do you sing the night long?" The reply would be, "We sing for freedom, for freedom. Let us go! Let us go!"

When Flora unbarred the door, four hundred little birds burst forth. Amazed, their Inspectress found herself snowed under with spools of cotton, spun during the night by the elder children. When the thread had been woven into cloth, it was dyed and embroidered. Finally, to the delight and admiration of the little spinners, Flora appeared in a dress that she owed to their spontaneous industry. The dress itself was cherished for the rest of her life by Flora as the garment in which she wished to pass from the corporeal world, a wish that was ultimately fulfilled.

It was not only her pupils who wished to protect Mrs Steel from her secret enemies. Rumour having spread that she might be in danger of assassination, a self-appointed guard of women would come to keep a night watch. Additionally, a friend in a Baluchi regiment offered the protection of a sergeant and four men, but Flora stoutly refused. She believed that her enemies were not only physically cowardly, but scared of the inquiry which would undoubtedly follow such a startling event as the murder of a British female educational officer. When the scandal finally broke, Flora was still living alone and undaunted in the *Bari dari*.

The man responsible for clearing up the affair, which had cast a sinister shadow over the University, was a Judge of the Chief Court of Lahore, Baden Henry Powell, elder half-brother of the founder of the Boy Scout movement. When Powell came across indisputable evidence of corruption, action was at last taken, a commission of inquiry from outside the province being set up. Evidence was recorded on oath, so that Flora underwent a grilling which lasted for four hours. At the end of the examination, with the scandal proved and herself vindicated, Flora found that she was hungrier than ever before in her life.

There seemed reason to believe that the Indian official who had offered the sapphire ring to the School Inspectress was much involved in the cycle of corruption. Flora realized that, had she not felt a suspicious dislike to the man himself, she might have even contemplated accepting what had seemed at the time a relatively harmless present to gain good will. In which case she could hardly have expected that her evidence would be believed. It was a European who appeared to the commission to be the principal culprit, but Flora, judging by her own experience, suspected that he might have been the victim of bribery and subsequent blackmail.

The happy ending, from Flora's point of view, included the sadness of losing the Eden of *Bara dari*, and presumably the family of affectionate squirrels. Before she rejoined Henry Steel however, the new Lieutenant Governor of the Punjab insisted that she should be invited to Government House, Simla, as the guest of the Viceroy, Lord Dufferin. Although she resented the idea that she needed any rehabilitation, Flora entered with her usual spirit into getting up theatricals. Her favourite performance as the Infant Phenomenon, with her round pink cheeks a perfect type-casting, was such a success with the courtly Lord Dufferin that he nearly fell off his chair in laughing.

Henry Steel, his wife wrote, had never liked Government service. His dislike, she feared, had been increased by the frequency of Flora's own scuffles with the authorities. Steel's retirement was due on May 1st, 1889. Mabel Steel had come out for a brief visit to her parents during the previous cold weather. The briefness of the visit was dictated by the precision with which her father had made his plans for departure. Naturally, Flora herself had her farewells to make, particularly to the schools where her most constructive work had been done. Tears must have been shed over the garlands without which no arrival or departure of moment can take place in India, but the tears were fewer than might have been expected. This was no reflection on the departing School Inspectress. Three hundred veiled women had gathered at the railway station to do Flora honour, but they were so excited at finding themselves in such an emancipated situation that weeping was kept at bay.

Two hours after his pension became due, Henry Steel, with his wife and daughter boarded a P & O liner, bound for retirement and home. He was for years haunted by a nightmare, fortunately only a nightmare, that the Accountant-General would inexorably summon him back to India to serve an additional fortnight. This horror could have only been increased by the thought of the shindy that Flora would have created, had the long arm of Government attempted to recapture its only too thankfully retired servant.

VIII

Flora's Indian Harvest

If Flora had enjoyed her success in entertaining Lord Dufferin, she was less than enthusiastic on the subject of the charitable activity for which Lady Dufferin, the Vicereine, is principally remembered. The Zenana Mission, which sent female nurses and doctors to tend those behind the curtains, has been celebrated by Kipling in a moving poem, describing the gratitude of the patients. Flora gave it as her opinion that such a scheme was ill-judged. From her experience its effect was to buttress the system of purdah, which would otherwise have broken down when the benefits of medical science became obvious to men and women alike.

Flora held this view, in spite of knowing that much of the opposition to abandoning purdah, even in cases of life and death, came from the women themselves. Matriarchs, who ruled the tangled generations below them, feared threats to their supremacy. Their lowliest subjects, the poor widows of the family, even in their slavery had the knowledge that they belonged to a recognized stratum in the female community, some protection from whatever demons awaited them in the world outside.

For twenty years Flora had been professionally concerned with problems that were often insoluble from the complexity of the characters involved. Her husband had served faithfully, leaving green things growing in places which had been formerly dusty wilderness. He had quit India with nothing but relief. Flora's temperament had led her to a deeper commitment. Freed from duties, she now gathered her harvest into sheaves. Errors she felt she might have made, but she also found aspects of her own conduct of which she could approve. She had learnt to read, it will be remembered, from Thomas à Kempis. His maxim, 'Whether men think well or ill

61

of thee, thou art not therefore another man,' had always appealed to Flora. She had a nature to set a value on her own opinion of herself, not to be upset by the ill-thinking of others.

Among the memories of the times she had been of positive use, Flora recalled that she had been the person to tell the British police officers that, in the Punjab, a woman with no sons giving birth to a female infant would expose the baby outside the village. If the unhappy daughter was carried off by jackals, it was believed that the next conception would inevitably be male. Whether the authorities took any steps following this revelation Flora did not say. On the contrary she dwelt in some detail on an occasion when it was necessary actually to search for a female child. As Vice-President of the 'Victoria Female Orphan Asylum' it was her job to find an orphaned girl for the opening ceremony. The Institution was not popular being financed by moneylenders, a class universally detested, as a propitiatory act towards Government in celebration of Queen Victoria's assumption of the title of Empress of India.

It was with difficulty that a female child was at last discovered who could be considered to qualify. Her father was indeed dead. Her mother, reputed to be what Flora called "an evil walker", might be considered to be so morally. Having procured, as it were, a moral orphan, preparations went forward. Flora found herself in another awkward spot when the local poet gave her an advance reading of his verses in celebration of the event. His English was enthusiastic rather than subtle, so Flora thought it right to try to get a flowery compliment with a double meaning modified. The compliment was directed at the Secretary-to-Government. Knowing Flora's stormy relations with this official, she must have been only too delighted when the poet stuck to his original expression.

At the ceremony Henry Steel, who had an endearing tendency to *fou rire*, nearly broke down when the poet read out the line, "Likewise the moon-faced Secretary-to-Government, whose cheek puts the whole Punjab to shame." Applause greeted the name of Government rather than the only too appropriate acclaim of the secretary, but before the poem had wound its way through the praise of the new Orphan Asylum, the whole festival was blotted out by an electrical dust storm.

On the many occasions when Flora had clashed with Government she had usually held her own, the character of an Infant Phenomenon sometimes merging into that of an Enfant Terrible. There was, however, one instance when she reluctantly refused an invitation which might have led to trouble, for which she could have been

62

fairly blamed. The invitation itself was a particular compliment, coming as it did from two teachers at a Hindu school for whom Flora had a strong affection. The teachers were an aunt and niece, both widows, both leading lives dedicated to the sanctity of their condition and their work. Exceptionally respected, these widows were regarded as holy women whose conduct brought a blessing on their home.

Nevertheless, in spite of their deep piety, the aunt and niece were prepared to dress Flora as one of themselves, in order that she could go with them to Benares. Here, in her disguise as a pilgrim widow, Flora would be able to see the inside of Visheswa's Temple, together with other holy sights prohibited to a woman of her race. Confident though she was of carrying out the impersonation, any strangeness of accent being passed off as the speech of a widow from the Afghan frontier, Flora refused. She felt that she would have been totally in the wrong had a row followed her literal unveiling. For once Government had had an escape from one of Mrs Steel's hand-grenades.

There were rewards also both for solving the problems of her fellow-countrymen, and for mothering young soldiers, many of whom could break down and weep in an agony of homesickness. At one Christmas Day dinner she expressed her longing for a snipe in terms so excessive that the subalterns of the Royal Artillery mess, who were her guests, took immediate action. They went on a shoot with such success that they were able to lay twenty-one brace of snipe on Flora's breakfast table. As a Boxing Day greeting it would be difficult to equal, but it was also a gesture of gratitude for her care and sympathy.

On the dark side, there were tragedies that stayed in Flora's memory, not ones that she could have averted, but still poignant to look back upon. Perhaps it was the loss of her first baby that made her especially sensitive to the shadow of death that hovered ever near during her years in India. On her second visit to Kashmir the District Officer had made superb arrangements for her comfort, including goats to be available at every sixth mile in case her convalescent appetite needed to be tempted with milk. Tortured by gout and arthritis, the District Officer had no wife to cosset him as he cosseted Mrs Steel. He told her, as a sad joke, that he had no wish to go to Heaven, for he knew that he would, inevitably, have gout on his wings. Within a year he put the matter to the test, dying by his own hand.

Sudden illness would strike, causing anxious days until the fever broke, or fears of more lethal disease were catastrophically fulfilled.

Sometimes the medical men disagreed, with tragic results. One doctor, in charge of fifteen hundred convicts digging the Chenab canal, was determined to confute his chief's diagnosis of epidemic pneumonia among the prisoners. He succumbed to typhus from doing too many post mortems, making his point in a ghastly fashion.

A weary colleague brought the news to Flora, together with the apprehension that the canal officer's wife might also be smitten with the same killer disease. Henry Steel read the burial service over the dead doctor, keeping quarantine away from home in the *dak* bungalow, while the woman's fever broke and the peril was past. Meanwhile Flora, herself a contact, waited among the shrubs that her husband had planted, cadadiums, yuccas, crotons, flowering in bland imperviousness to human crises.

Saddest of all was the loss of the doctor who had been Flora's earliest friend when, as a bride, she had begun her Indian adventure. With him the Steels had shared Beethoven, Scottish reels, border ballads, the domestic disasters and jokes of their early days, the doctor throwing his feet into the air while he shouted with laughter. Subsequently he had married a charming wife, only to lose her at the birth of their second child. When the Steels paid him a visit, he still seems to have been living in the big house at Ludhiana which they had all shared. His children had been sent home, so a return to the music and laughter of former days was an acute pleasure to the lonely doctor.

With the mail phaeton at the door, their host begged Henry to leave Flora with him for a few days longer, her presence bringing an indescribable comfort to the big empty house. Promising that she should come back and stay for a fortnight, Henry, faced with a dinner party that evening in a house forty miles away, felt obliged to take his wife home. Cholera, the ever-waiting slayer, struck in the night, when there was no friend to comfort the forlorn widower. Flora had often noticed the philosophical resignation with which Indians faced the threat of cholera, compared with the panic which its imminence caused among Europeans. Flora's own evidence shows that, useless though this terror might be, it was far from unreasonable.

Flora's artist's eye was not only used for recording the scenes around her. When her husband was attacked for delays in completing his returns, she checkmated the Financial Commissioner by drawing a coloured chart which showed the situation at a glance. In shades of pale pink deepening to crimson, the chart demonstrated incontestably that the worst bottle-neck was in the Financial Commissioner's own office. The same colour effect, on a chart, proved Steel to be right in his demand that a new railway line should deviate to open up a large wheat-growing district. This latter chart made such an impression that copies, as an example of what might be done, were distributed throughout the Punjab.

As she sailed from Bombay, watching the splendours and squalors of the city that had been part of Catherine of Braganza's dowry fade into an infinitely mysterious blue mist, Flora brooded on the false air of homogeneity which that mist gave to the landscape. Little as she felt she had learnt in her years in India, she could at least tell herself that she had stood on the edge of an ancient mystery. Never hesitating to explore such mysteries as might come her way, Flora was skilful in hoarding her experiences. They remained on mental deposit until she needed them to illuminate her writing.

It was, however, practical matters that concerned her in the second of the two books she published before her husband's retirement. The book was a joint enterprise, shared with a friend, Grace Gardiner, its title, *The Complete Indian Housekeeper and Cook*, stating exactly what the book set out to be. There is a rather unamiable remark in the *Dictionary of National Biography* to the effect that neither author was renowned as a housewife, but in her case members of Flora's family declare this criticism to be untrue. She herself wrote that her wedding cakes were iced with professional expertise, and that her scones were equally famous.

Mrs Gardiner's personality comes across indirectly, and her domestic qualifications can, at best, only be deduced. If the subject was not a sad one, there would be an air of comedy when the authors disagree over the problem of bringing up the children of English parents serving in India. Separate chapters, written from opposite points of view, demonstrate each author's unshakeable faith in her own rightness.

The Complete Indian Housekeeper and Cook was dedicated to the public for whose use it was designed, "The English Girls to whom fate may assign the task of being House-Mothers in Our Eastern Empire". The date of the first edition is given as 1888. During its compilation, Flora could not have guessed that Rudyard Kipling, then a young reporter sweating through the hot nights, would emerge as the interpreter of that Empire for which she was supplying a survival manual.

Although claiming to be self-educated, Flora was entirely capable of using the tools of academic workmanship when researching for her books. Her husband's sister had married Henry Nettleship, a professor at Oxford University. This gave Flora, when on leave, an opportunity to check facts in Oxford libraries. She loved her brother-in-law, who introduced her to the great men of those days, Pater, Jowett, Ruskin, Pattison. He also introduced her to Goldwin Smith, at a moment when Flora was preoccupied with research into the care of cows.

The words of the introduction flabbergasted Goldwin Smith, former Regius Professor of Modern History. "Oh Smith" (said Professor Nettleship) "This is my sister-in-law, she wants to know the normal temperature of a cow; no doubt you'll be able to tell her."

Incidentally, whether or not deriving from Goldwin Smith, Mrs Steel's advice on cow-keeping has recently been approved by a young mother deeply experienced in Indian house-keeping.

Lewis Nettleship, brother of the Professor, was found even more congenial by Flora. He died in an accident on Mont Blanc, but he had already opened to her new avenues of philosophical speculation. Ida, sister of these brilliant brothers, carried her study of art to such an extreme that she married, as his first wife, Augustus John. Her last child, from whose birth she did not recover, was later to play a part in Flora's grandson's life, and in her own theatrical productions.

Flora's writing was not limited to recounting folk tales and expounding political economy. She thought it unwise of the editor of Indian Public Opinion to invite her to write leaders during his own illness, but years later she was gratified to find that the legal reforms she had advocated had been adopted by tortoise-like Government. Such assignments must, in any case have been valuable to Flora as discipline in writing. She must also have been thankful for her memory's retention of the sights she had seen, after the irreplaceable loss of her Indian sketches. The portfolio left at home for safety, disappeared, taking with it the record of her delight in the marvels of India. She could only fall back on what was, fortunately, a remarkably faithful inward eye.

IX

The Writer Emerges

Subconsciously, Flora may have known that she had not said a final goodbye to India, for she was plagued neither by the nightmares which haunted her husband, nor by the withdrawal symptoms of retirement. A Highland shoot, remote from shops, immediately tested her powers of organization. She found these powers to be stretched, after years of attendance from Indian servants, who could at least be relied upon to carry out a given order. In Scotland she thought her domestics' tendency to follow their own will an exasperating handicap to good household economy. Eighteen guests had to be fed, thirty-six pairs of boots to be polished. When the boot boy chanced to be incapacitated, it was the hostess who cleaned the boots.

It would certainly have taken more than three dozen pairs of muddy boots to suppress Flora's creativity, but it is surprising that it actually needed a friend to suggest that she might turn her Indian experiences into saleable goods. From the inscriptions in presentation copies of her books, it seems that the friend who urged her to develop her gifts was Richard Gillies Hardy, an Indian Civilian who rose to be Commissioner of Lucknow.

"*Lâl*", the story with which Flora broke into the world of London publishing, was a gleaning from the days when she had followed her husband through the fertile river lands. The immemorial problems to be dealt with were still unchanged when, in 1930, the author Philip Mason arrived on his first ICS appointment. Mason's account of his initial inspection reads like an echo of the days when Flora went into camp. A good ICS officer still watched the treacherous ebb and flow of the rivers, and learnt to know his district from riding and shooting over it, as Henry Steel had done half a century before.

Throughout the story, "*Lâl*" is illuminated by the colour notes of an artist, accustomed to look and remember. "It was after forcing my way through one of the tamarisk jungles that I came out on an open patch of rudely ploughed land, where a mixed crop of pulse and barley grew sturdily, outlining an irregular oval with a pale green carpet glistening with dew. In the centre a shallow pool of water still testified to past floods, and from it a purple heron winged its flight, lazily craning its painted neck against the sky . . ."

"Take the bridle from his honour's pony," cried a venerable pantaloon breathlessly. "Let the steed of the Lord of the Universe eat his fill. Is not this the field of Lâl? . . ."

"A minute more, and my pony's nose was well down on the wet, sweet tufts of vetch, and I was asking for the first time, 'Who is Lâl?'"

This question is never really answered for "*Lâl*" is a teasing story. The male narrator is not even sure in the end, whether this will-o'-the wisp, who purports to have been buried, has really died. It is even doubtful if he has ever lived in a human sense. The river Indus, deceitfully changeful, has, it seems, deprived Lâl of the field where the officer of Government's pony could snatch a meal of pulse and barley. On the other hand, the river itself is the hunting ground for Lâl, which offers him crocodile as prey. Having slit the reptile's belly, Lâl feeds himself and his poorest friends on the sun-dried meat, but he remains, always, an invisible Robin Goodfellow of the river lands.

As her friend, R. G. Hardy, had suggested, Flora began by sending the story to minor magazines. Refusals were not discouraging to one of her fighting temperament. She treated them as a challenge to set her sights higher. Her instinct was proved to be right, for success came at her first approach to a major periodical. Mowbray Morris of *Macmillan's Magazine*, immediately recognizing the lively originality of "*Lâl*", accepted the story and asked for more. He addressed his letters to F. A. Steel Esq., not unreasonably as the story was told by a man. Only after three years did he discover his mistake. In the meantime he had had his ears boxed through the post by the author, for making an alteration in a story which *Macmillan's Magazine* had published. Assumedly still from a male writer, the protest was of a strength beyond Mowbray Morris's editorial experience.

For the rest of her life, death alone cutting short her literary career, Flora found no difficulty in marketing her wares. An occasional publishing scuffle she found positively invigorating. Usually on the winning side, she was prepared to accept a suggested change of title for her first novel. Originally she had chosen *Legacy Duty*, but agreed to the alteration, *Miss Stuart's Legacy*. Possibly the former title displeased Macmillan by its suggestion of a handbook on inheritance taxes.

Miss Stuart's Legacy may have been Flora's first novel, but she had already come to understand the importance of an opening scene that would catch the reader's imagination. The heroine makes her appearance on the platform of a small railway station in the Punjab. The train of her arrival has crossed with the down train, bearing the Homeward Mail and an English family going home on leave. No-one has come to meet Belle Stuart, but on the platform, by chance, is Philip Marsden. He, after many vicissitudes, is to become the accepted lover of the heroine.

Exchanges on the subject of the newly arrived girl set the scene. The Homeward Mail steams out, carrying with it parents who, after the pleasures of their leave will return without their children. Belle, arrived to join her father and his Eurasian second wife, finds herself dependent on Philip Marsden to send her on the next stage of her journey. By the time he has done so, it is clear to the reader that Colonel Stuart, still off-stage, is a drunken gambler. Even clearer is the vision of the Indian dawn, sparkling air overhead, while on sordid earth a pariah dog licks axle grease from the train's wheels and carrion crows sit agape on the telegraph wires.

With the emergence of Flora Annie Steel as a novelist, it is important to mention a lucid and detailed study of her works by one who has the advantage of seeing them from an Indian point of view. Its author, Mrs Daya Patwardhan, a distinguished scholar, professor and PhD, was, when her book appeared, head of the Department of English at Khalsa College, Bombay. She called her study of Mrs Steel's works *A Star of India*, publishing it herself in Bombay in 1963. The title chosen was in memory of the brooch of assorted jewels, which had been a token of love from the people of Kasur.

Feeling that Mrs Steel's remarkable understanding of the Indian peoples might well be forgotten since her death thirty years earlier, Mrs Patwardhan set herself to analyse this understanding with scholarly thoroughness. *A Star of India* tells of Flora's career in India as a collector of folk tales, a novelist and an educationalist. Its appendices include a chronological list of Mrs Steel's works, with their subjects, Indian or British. In addition there is an analysis of the short stories with the ideas and scenes that were their inspiration.

The author's task was complicated by the fact that Independence had cleft the sub-continent into two uneven parts, separating by a new frontier some of the stations in the Punjab to which Henry Steel had been posted. Faced with the difficulty of handling the many tragic events which had darkened the setting up of the new states, Mrs Patwardhan sensibly decided to concentrate on India as Flora had known it. She considered that already in *Miss Stuart's Legacy* the author showed an instinctive understanding and grasp of the varieties of peoples to be found among "the teeming millions of India".

Teeming also well describes the quantity of characters to appear in *Miss Stuart's Legacy*. The development of the action depends largely on the gullibility of the heroine, whose mixing of blind loyalty with an awkward conscience gets everyone into trouble. She marries John Raby, a sinister Civilian, who, by crooked means, has learnt that she is an heiress. It is in writing of this marriage that Flora subscribes to a convention of the Victorian novel concerning physical relations between the sexes. This convention may have inhibited her when writing of Europeans, but, as will be seen, she set it aside when she came to write of Indian love and marriage.

To explain this convention it must be remembered that here was an age when contraception was seldom practised or even comprehended. There were also strict rules as to what words might not appear on the printed page. For their part novelists knew readers would assume that love-making would almost certainly be followed by conception. Indeed for a child to be born was for most novelists the only means by which it could be indicated that physical relations had certainly taken place. Equally the career of a heroine married to a villain might be handicapped by the presence of a living child. Consequently, small graves abound in nineteenth century fiction. To one of these is consigned the child of Belle Stuart and John Raby.

Flora had had the harrowing experience of losing her child at birth, and she put much of her own suffering into her first novel. She also used her holidays in the mountains as a background for a minor military campaign. Miss Stuart and her admirer Philip Marsden have noble characters, but it is the husband, John Raby, fundamentally brave in spite of his crooked ways, who catches the reader's interest.

Raby is finally a victim of his own greed, which has involved him in the politics of irrigation. The dam he has had built to water a profitable indigo crop, adversely affects the fields of the neighbouring village. The villagers sabotage the dam, Raby dying in the attack. There have been intrigues among the Indian business community which have led indirectly to Raby's death. These intrigues and the complicated fortunes of Belle's Eurasian step brothers and sisters have a vitality that is sometimes lacking in the episodes which concern the pure-bred Europeans. Dealing with characters which she saw at one remove, Flora wrote with the confidence of one who had found her métier and rejoiced in it.

When Mowbray Morris accepted "*Lâl*", the first story sent him by Flora, it was not merely with the acumen of an editor whose nose twitched on scenting a new talent. He was peculiarly well qualified to judge the merits of the story, for he had been Art Editor on that famous paper the *Allahabad Pioneer*. He was, in consequence, one of the few contacts in literary journalism available to Rudyard Kipling when, in the autumn of 1889, the latter arrived to lay siege to London.

Almost immediately *Macmillan's Magazine* published the *Ballad of East and West*, the firm of Macmillan remaining ever after Kipling's publisher. From this it can be seen that Mowbray Morris had every reason to rely on his own judgement when he recognized that F. A. Steel Esq, as he addressed the author, had a rare appreciation of Indian life. He must also have considered that the market had not been entirely cornered by the genius of Kipling.

Owing to the enormous success of his Indian stories, it can have been no surprise to Flora when a reviewer wrote "this story is either by Kipling or Diabolus". She quotes this tribute to *Harvest*, a story about ill-advised changes in the land laws of the Punjab, with perhaps a touch of malice. She was writing her memoirs with the determination that there should be no unwarranted intrusions into her *Garden of Fidelity*. Rudyard Kipling signally failed to gain full admission, being only allowed what might be called a glance over the hedge. Flora had lived to see the Infant Phenomenon of literature become a sage honoured by Oxford University. She leaves the impression that, had she been offered the rôle of Kipling or Diabolus, it would have been the latter, devilish as it was, that she would have chosen.

Belle Stuart, newly arrived in India, might be considered the sort of girl for whom Flora and Grace Gardiner had written *The Complete Indian Housekeeper and Cook*. With *The Potter's Thumb* her next Indian novel, Flora plunged deeper into the life of the sub-continent. The intrigues among a former ruling family are only equalled by those of the raffish racing set at Simla. Here the beautiful but unreliable Mrs Boynton makes hay among her admirers. Irrigation plays an even more important and sinister part than in *Miss Stuart's Legacy*, but perhaps the best scene describes an attempt to rig a race. This is defeated by red paint from a marker being detected on the wrong knee of a crooked rider. Race riding and irrigation were subjects in which Henry Steel was expert, his knowledge surely supplying food for Flora's imagination.

71

Once again in *The Potter's Thumb* there is a family of the kind that Flora knew well from her days among the schools for Eurasians. With the unselfconsciousness of the period, Flora referred to these as her schools for black-and-tans, particularly cherishing the exotic names that prevailed among the children. She so liked Elflida Norma that she used it on two occasions. The Elflida Norma of *The Potter's Thumb* is an Eurasian girl who decides that marriage with a dissipated princeling offers more of a future than she could find in her own world. She has the sense to make a pact with her husband's mistress, a powerful figure both in her own city and in the demimonde of Simla. A Swiss chalet is tacked onto the ancient tower of the palace. Here Elflida Norma settles down to breed children, with the approval of the prince's mistress. Should the prince succumb to his way of life the widow's pension will increase in ratio to the number of children he leaves behind, and of this pension the mistress is assured of her cut.

It should, incidentally, be recorded that a critic, author of a prize essay on the subject of Anglo-Indian literature, considered *The Potter's Thumb* to be Mrs Steel's greatest achievement. Writing in 1908, Edward Farley Oaten praised the devious Mrs Boynton as the equal of Kipling's Mrs Hauksbee. Oaten also considered that "within the limits of a single page" the highest and lowest notes of life's octave had been touched. The winner of The Le Bas Prize Essay for 1907 gave it as his opinion that Mrs F. A. Steel was "perhaps the greatest novelist, in the strictest sense of the word," of whom Anglo-Indian literature could boast.

The subject set for the Le Bas Essay, expanded by Oaten into a book, had been portentous. The entrants were required to give "An Appreciation of the chief Productions of Anglo-Indian Literature in the Domain of Fiction, Poetry, the Drama, Satire, and Belles-Lettres, during the Eighteenth and Nineteenth Centuries, with an Estimate of the Chief Writers in those Spheres, and a Consideration of the specially Anglo-Indian Features of the Literature." To come top in her own class in such a far-flung survey must have gratified Flora, particularly as *The Potter's Thumb* owed much to her earliest experiences in the Punjab and at Simla.

In the autumn of 1894, soon after the publication of *The Potter's Thumb*, Flora sailed alone for Bombay on a venture that was to place her in the forefront of interpreters of the Indian scene. Telling of the beginning of this journey, Flora for once slightly relaxed a hold over her emotions. A very old friend, she wrote, had recently sent her a lengthy letter. To this he added a postscript, "By the way, I wa-married the other day." Flora's riposte was equally in character. Her letter occupied itself only with news and views, but in her turn she added a postscript, "By the way, I died the day before yesterday."

The old friend Colonel (subsequently Major-General) Malcolm Nicolson, son of a father distinguished in the Indian Army, was himself famous for his proficiency in Indian languages. Nicolson's marriage, so casually mentioned, had in fact taken place somewhat earlier than Flora had given her readers to suppose. She also fell into the trap of adding an "h" to the surname of her old friend. Flora had never met the bride, born Adela Florence Cory, who had not yet become famous, even notorious, as a writer of erotic verse. Mrs Nicolson's poems, originally accepted as those of a male writer, were to appear under the name of "Laurence Hope", the best-known purporting to celebrate Indian conceptions of passion.

Although there were sceptics who suggested that these *Indian Love Lyrics* owed more to Swinburne than to a Vedic marriage hymn, their success was immense. The Temple Bells Rang at a myriad concerts, together with the invocation of Pale Hands beside the Shalimar, and the desire to be Less than the Dust beneath the Chariot Wheels of the Beloved. The poems were also popular for heightening the emotions on more private occasions.

That Laurence Hope provided some small change for love transactions in the *beau monde* may be deduced from Anthony Glyn's biography of his grandmother, the novelist Elinor Glyn. This other high priestess of passion received a copy of *Indian Love Lyrics* as a rather obvious parting gift from Lord Alastair Innes-Ker, when he, a favourite admirer, was on the point of sailing for the land which had inspired the poems. Mrs Glyn's friend and close neighbour, Frances Countess of Warwick, valued the poems for more immediately practical purposes. Lady Warwick, mistress of King Edward VII, lived at Easton Lodge near Bishops Stortford, in whose garden was situated a strategically placed summer house. Its fittings included a copy of poems by Laurence Hope, thoughtfully provided as an adjunct to amorous encounters.

The Indian approach to love was not the only one to interest Laurence Hope. She also concerned herself with the question of that rather legendary privilege, *le droit de seigneur*. A poem was devoted to the meditation of a village maiden, betrothed to a suitable mate, but contemplating the prospect of surrendering her virginity to the lord of the manor with fears that can only be called unexpected. Sometime previously another village girl, sent to the castle on the same errand of surrender, had been returned by the lord like an unwanted present, the gift-wrapping still intact. This unravished bride had in due course given birth to a child whose loutishness showed it to be of the village rather than the castle.

The débâcle has filled Laurence Hope's heroine with apprehension that she might also be rejected, a thought that causes her to send out a mental appeal to the lord of the castle. It is not only the conscious beauty who feels the idea as an insult, she is determined that at least one of her children shall be nobly sired. With this in mind she has turned down her bethrothed's suggestion that they should ignore the priest's disapproval of couples who anticipate their marriage vows. Whatever subsequent goings-on at the castle, they might then be certain that their eldest child would be a joint production. (What the priest thought of *le droit de seigneur* is not recorded.) A twist is added to the story by the heroine's reflection that the noble family's behaviour with the girls of the village has been so profligate that she well may be half-sister to the present lord. Undeterred by this possibility of incest, she can only assure him that a moment's enjoyment on his side will provide her with satisfaction for life.

Although it contains material for a long novel the poem covers little more than two pages. Its plot has been recounted in detail because it is enjoyable to speculate what Flora would have made of such a story. She might have toned down the incestuous sexuality of the girl's meditations, but she would certainly have enjoyed handling in detail the panorama of which Laurence Hope gave only the outline.

Colonel Nicolson had chosen somewhat inexplicably to call his wife Violet, but nevertheless she adored him. He was more than twenty years older than his wife, who was considerably younger than Flora. Few women are unreservedly delighted when a congenial bachelor friend marries a wife younger than themselves. Flora was no exception. Even if her declaration that she had never been in love is respected, it does seem that she felt more warmly than was her custom towards Malcolm Nicolson. There is what might be called a literary sniff in her account of her first experience of Violet Nicolson's personality.

From her girlhood Flora had always made her own clothes, combining her own taste with a reasonable acceptance of the fashions of the moment. A photograph taken in 1897 at the time of her great public success shows her in a velvet gown over a white bodice tied at the neck, her hair still in the rough short cut she had favoured in Kashmir. Although extremes of décolletage were frowned on in conventional circles, some baring of the neck and bosom was expected in evening dress. Dress in the daytime was another matter. Even in the hottest climates decency and dread of sunburn ordinarily dictated that the neck should be covered. Flora accepted sunburn as a hazard of her life, but disapproved of the undue display of bare flesh with which Violet Nicolson presented her at their first meeting.

Together the new acquaintances drove through Bombay in an open carriage, the sunburnt little lady in the wide pith hat sitting beside a striking figure in a low-necked, short-sleeved pink satin dress. Omitting the colour, it is possible to get an idea of Mrs Nicolson's appearance from the frontispiece of her last book of poems *Indian Love*, published posthumously in 1905. The photograph was a study by G. C. Beresford, the original of M'Turk in Kipling's *Stalky and Co*. It is wildly different from the stiffly posed studio portrait of Flora. The subject's loose-necked dress, waves of hair and informal attitude might be accepted to-day as those of a contemporary sitter.

They were not accepted as agreeable by Flora when she drove beside Violet Nicolson through Bombay. As a rule Flora was too much occupied in observing the mysterious flow of Indian life to trouble herself about what those floating on its current might be thinking of her. Finely attuned to compliment or insult, she felt herself to be capable of dealing, unruffled, with either. On this daytime drive, however, she found herself acutely conscious of the dark eyes drawn to the outré get-up of her companion. It was not, she thought, a sight to sustain British prestige.

The end of the Nicolsons' story was tragically in keeping with the spirit of Laurence Hope's poems. Ten years after the drive through Bombay, General Nicolson died. He was buried in the graveyard of St Mary's Church, Madras, whose pale spire still keeps watch over three centuries of Christian dead. His widow expressed her feelings in an elegiac poem, dedicating her last book to Malcolm Nicolson.

> "Small joy was I to thee; before we met
> Sorrow had left thee all too sad to save.
> Useless my love—as vain as this regret
> That pours my hopeless life across thy grave."

Two months later, Violet Nicolson moved from poetry to action. She joined Nicolson in his grave, having committed, with poison, what can only be called *suttee*. Mrs Patwardhan has pointed out that Flora, on at least one occasion, confuses a woman who burns herself on her husband's funeral pyre with a woman who leads a saintly life, both being called a *suttee*. This was demonstrably a confusion impossible to Laurence Hope. If her poems had English harmonies that made their Indian pretensions slightly absurd, in her widowhood she did not hesitate to emulate the discarded custom of the land of her inspiration.

X

Return to Kasur

The novel with which Flora hit the jackpot was, she wrote, the result of a project that had been cooking in her mind ever since she had arrived in India. Indeed, on looking back over her life story, it seems possible that it germinated as far back as her nursery days when she had slashed at a doll called Nana Sahib. Throughout her time in India she had gathered much experience and understanding, but in the background there was always capricious Government with power to direct her husband's movements. On occasion Flora had fought the authorities to a standstill, but nonetheless she had had to take their whims into consideration. Leaving her husband and daughter to follow later, she returned to India in 1894. This time she arrived as a free agent, a writer whose work had been noticed and praised. Borne up by some early success, she arrived with a plan in her mind as well thought out as it was ambitious.

Although her position as an Inspector of Education had made Flora well known from Peshawar to Delhi, there was one place in particular to which she wished to return. She knew that here she would regain, as it were, the feel of Indian life. This place was, of course, the city of Kasur, where she had spent the first years of her Indian sojourn, learning to take steps to cross the barrier which separates East and West.

With the idea of testing the memories of those who had once been her friends, almost her subjects, Flora arrived unheralded and alone. Standing in the familiar dust at Kasur station, she was superciliously asked by the Bengali station master if she was "Mission lady", almost an insult to Mrs Steel's way of thinking. Restraining any manifestation of temper such as her father might have displayed, she announced herself as *Mem* Steel *sahiba*. The long memories of Indians for those they have learnt to admire and respect did the rest. Coolies appeared, among them the aged *bhisti* from bygone days, eager to transport Flora's trunk and bedding-roll. Between the lines of trees and flowers planted long before by Henry Steel, his wife was escorted in triumph to the *dak* bungalow.

Telling her old friends that this was no passing visit, she requested them to find her a house, which they promptly did. In a few hours she had settled down to a way of life, frugal but not uncomfortable when she had indented for a galvanized bath from Firozpur. Her primary object was to acquire copy, the plot of her novel depending on the fact that an Englishwoman should live, undetected, in an Indian house during the siege of Delhi.

Admittedly the siege was forty years in the past, but this made little difference to the immemorial pattern of Indian life. The warning call of the sweeper, raised so that ladies might retreat before a male presence, the less inhibited call of the water carrier, these cannot have altered down the centuries. While Flora lay awake, trying to accustom herself to the acrid smoke that rose at nightfall from the cooking fires of cow dung, the only voice from the modern world outside would be that of the bearer of a telegram, calling that there was "wire news" for the addressee.

Readers of Nirad C. Chaudhuri's *Continent of Circe* will have learnt how much of the life of Indian cities takes place on the roof. It was this life that Flora shared in the two months which she spent in Kasur. She gave alms, and medical advice, sometimes fifty patients came in the course of one day to ask for the latter, but listening was what she had come to do and listen she did. Wherever she went she heard the same disquieting story. There was unrest and discontent among all classes, which could be blamed on what, in fact, had been intended as steps to substitute more native participation for earlier despotic practices. Ignorant of the processes that were meant to protect them, the people complained that the law, the pleaders and the police took every opportunity to exact their own tribute from the bewildered victims of misplaced good-will. Even out in the country the peasants told the same tale, but here there were happy recollections of "the sahib who planted gardens". Of Henry Steel it might truly be said that,

> "Only the actions of the just
> Smell sweet and blossom in the dust."

Flora's own life in Kasur was filled with collecting material for her projected novel besides giving what medical help she could to her neighbours. Among the women she was continually struck by a lack of occupation and, inconsequently, by a lack of leisure. Petty incidents were magnified until they developed into quarrels, with always the element of sex to add pepper to the disputes. Priding herself on her unshockability, Flora learnt to accept aspects of Hindu life and customs which she believed would appal her fellow countrywomen. The ritual to celebrate the onset of a daughter's puberty would not, she fancied, be regarded except with horror among European women bred to a different standard of modesty.

This attitude towards menstruation was not always so entirely alien to Europeans as Flora seems to have supposed. The first Duke of Wellington told Lord Stanhope, *à propos* of King Louis XVIII's habit of saying "mess i eurs", that the King had not hesitated to convey the improved prospects for a royal heir to his court. "Mess i eurs", (the King had declared) "Je vous annonce que Madame la Duchesse de Berri est femme," an essentially Hindu approach to the sexual development of a nephew's wife.

After two months on her roof at Kasur, Flora completed her period of re-Indianisation by spending a week with a Hindu family in Lahore. Here was no romantic garden house such as she had enjoyed in the great days of her war with the University. She slept in a narrow, dark little room, or rather she struggled to do so, while the life of the household stormed round her, there being no fixed time for sleep in an Indian home. The noise was augmented by the incessant playing of a portable harmonium, the performers asking the *mem-sahiba* to identify what tune was intended. Flora, musically educated in a classical tradition, was never able to hazard anything except "God Save the Queen."

Accustomed as she was to making the best of things, Flora felt that one week was about the limit of her endurance. Her hosts were only anxious to be kind, but the household was ruled by a widowed sister of the owner, before whom nieces and nephews trembled. Far removed from the dedicated nun-like widows of whom Flora had written with such admiration, this dictatorial aunt kept everybody off-balance by the sudden insistence on taboos which Flora suspected were often invented for her own power purposes. When a curry of carrots was beginning to bubble, the tartar would announce that in a house where she made the rules, carrots must never be eaten on a Friday. Only by refusing to heat the bath water for the widow's obligatory morning ablutions could the family, when exasperated beyond bearing, control the tyrant, she having a horror of cold water.

Calling a truce with her old enemy the Punjab Government, Flora had asked permission to examine the sealed boxes of confidential papers relating to the Mutiny, which she knew to exist in the Delhi offices. After a bureaucratic pause, she received leave to examine all she wished, with the proviso that her discretion and loyalty were, it was understood, totally to be relied upon. Flora had long been pondering the framework of her novel, so that she was seeking background rather than sensational discoveries. The permission's qualification struck her as particularly comic as she was allowed to take the boxes, unsupervised, to her hotel sitting room. Here she sat, suffering from a hideous cold brought on by the chilly weather, with, as she said, nothing to prevent her from warming herself by a fire of burning records.

No-one before Flora had had the influence or the initiative to examine these archives. Of this unique opportunity she took the fullest advantage. Unhelped by the photographic methods of a later age, every fact she wanted had to be noted by herself, with the knowledge that a strong force of military historians would be waiting, fully armed, to shoot her down over the smallest slips. Subsequent writers knew her as an authority to be relied upon. More than one has absorbed from Flora the material for best sellers which might be called the grand-children of *On the Face of the Waters*.

The fascination of the research, if wearing, was spell-binding. Secret messages might be found concealed in quills, and in one case even in a piece of *chupatti*, that unleavened bread whose baking had had a mysterious influence on the spread of the Mutiny. Flora drove herself into a physical collapse, but she was not for long incapacitated. On her recovery she began the field work for her novel, knowing that the details of Delhi's geography would be essential to the book's realism.

She found the byways of the city of the Mughals to be a maze of sophistication compared to the relative simplicity of friendly Kasur. Flora prowled the streets, but she also took every opportunity to visit those who claimed to be descended from the Mughal Dynasty. Fascinated by the contradictions of genius and licentiousness among the Mughals, she eventually wrote four historical novels based on the generations which began with Babar, continued with Akbar, Humayan, and Jahangir, to end with Shahjahan. The descendants of these magnificent rulers Flora found to be, in only too many cases, text book examples of decadence.

Forty years earlier, with the exile of Bahadur Shah, the last shadowy Mughal Emperor, the new rulers, the British, had agreed to continue the pensions by which a multitude of female dependants kept starvation at arm's length. The pensions, it was arranged, could be handed *en bloc* to whatever male happened to be head of any particular branch of a family. This scheme showed a naïve lack of consideration for what Flora called the Muslim's attitude to their womenkind in business matters. As a result of the system, Flora found an elderly, half-blind lady, reduced to the despised spinning-wheel for her support. Her pension, whose non-payment had brought her to these straits, was supposedly passed to her by male relatives, since she had been originally seen as too young and flighty to receive it direct.

Four decades later, when youth and flightiness had indubitably fled, the control of this pension had come to rest in the hands of a *nawab*, to whose fingers it appeared to stick. Flora may have disapproved of him as certainly decadent and very possibly corrupt, but as a character she found him a useful type. Her artist's eye recorded the dyes and scents applied to preserve an air of rakish youth. Additionally, she noted that the golden yellow of the nawab's satin coatee was a close match with the jaundiced colour of his face.

Her mind now well-stocked with material, Flora settled down to write the book which, in its day, was the definitive novel of the Indian Mutiny. Settling down is not, however, an accurate description of the condition in which she was obliged to work. She had returned home to a rented house in the Highlands, continually full of guests and kindred. If Mrs Steel did not clean the boots daily, she had to supervise the house-keeping, giving portions to an ever hungry crowd of sporting visitors. Seldom was she able to write for more than two hours without interruption for the meals at which eighteen might be seated round the table.

Emerging in a trancelike state from composing a powerful death scene in her Mutiny novel, she found her guests already engaged in tackling the good food with Highland appetites. It was then that Henry Steel made one of his few recorded domestic criticisms. Why, he inquired gently, was the cucumber bitter? With her mind still occupied by the gallant end of the seductress Alice Gissing, Flora was for once without words. The mental leap was too great for her to arrive back in the present, where bitterness in cucumbers could be explained by the steel knife used to cut them.

XI

On the Face of the Waters

In addition to years of gestation, the novel whose composition had blocked the bitterness of cucumbers from Flora's mind had also long possessed its title. *On the Face of the Waters* was drawn from the reiterated "God knows. He sent a breath into the world," with which uneducated Indians would answer inquiries as to the origin of the Great Rebellion. With this thought to back the experience of twenty years, she dived into her story as she dived into the ancient swimming bath at Kasur. Her opening chapter immediately lands the reader in a scene of exotic outrage. The menagerie of the deposed King of Oudh, is being offered at auction. The atmosphere is one of doom, increased by the auctioneer's cry of "Going! Going! Gone!", which gives this first chapter its title. Elephants, fighting rams, even tigers, are proving, in auctioneering terms, hard to move. Earlier the dead stock, the King's carriages, had been sold cheaply to the followers of the new British power. In desperation, the aggressively cockney auctioneer begins to sell off the parrots, which have at least the recommendation of being edible.

Watching the sale is a pair on horseback, British, but in the woman's case far removed from the idea, already becoming stereotyped, of the conventional *memsahib*. Alice Gissing, in spite of her pretty baby looks, has a rubbery toughness of character, a cool realism towards life and, additionally, unshakeable physical courage. Always with a male escort, she teases Major Erlton, at present her most favoured admirer, into paying the outrageous price of fifty rupees for a dejected cockatoo. Grief-stricken, the underbidder declares the bird to be really his. The cockatoo had only been lent to the King as a tutor to the royal aviary. Indeed at intervals the bird rouses itself from shrivelled lethargy to give the cry of the Faith "Deen! Deen! Futteh Mahomed."

At this inopportune moment, Mrs Erlton drives by on her way to a Lenten service. She clings all the more to her religion now that she has sent her son to England. This separation has not been from the usual mistrust of the Indian climate, but to keep the boy from his father's influence. Major Erlton, unfortunately, is a man of unreliable character, adding riding crooked races to his pursuit of Mrs Gissing.

With a mixture of contempt for Mrs Erlton's chilly piety and pity for her inability to keep the interest of her own husband, Alice Gissing presents Mrs Erlton with the fanatical cockatoo. The bird's cry is part of the general atmosphere of ill-omen in the spring of 1856. The day of "Going! Going! Gone!" ends with gunfire, the shooting of the beasts who have found no buyers. Kate Erlton is shaken by the shots and accompanying howls, but she is even more appalled when her husband returns home in a state of angry discomposure. He has been accused on strong evidence of riding yet another crooked race.

This contretemps introduces into the story a Scotchman, bearing the name of Greyman, but in reality a former Army officer called Jim Douglas. Having left the Service under a cloud, he has been making a living by training the deposed King's horses, with a bit on the side from riding races on his own account. The annexation of Oudh has thrown him out of work, along with many others who depended on the dissolute court of Lucknow for subsistence. It was therefore vital that he should have won the race in which Major Erlton managed to defeat him by foul riding. Flora does not specify exactly what form Major Erlton's cheating took, but she used the incident of a rigged race in more than one book. If Henry Steel's light weight and good horsemanship led him to success on the race-course, it also must have enabled him to supply his wife with details from racing's seamier side.

In an attempt to avert her husband's public disgrace, Kate Erlton sends for the man she only knows as Greyman, living by his wits and guarding a dubious secret in his past. This knowledge gives her confidence that the diamonds she has been hoarding to pay for her son's education will be an adequate bribe to persuade Greyman to drop his accusation against her husband. She finds that she has misjudged a man she had taken for an unscrupulous adventurer. For his part he finds her cool grey eyes disturbingly like the eyes of the woman for whom he has wrecked his career. Perhaps as a result of his likeness, Jim Douglas finally agrees to accept Kate's appeal for mercy on account of her son's future. When they part the reader may already suspect that they are to meet again with increasing interest in each other.

Greyman's, or rather Douglas's, crossing of the barrier between Indian and Europe has not been limited to race riding and horse coping. He has an Indian mistress, bought at the beginning of her career as a prostitute, now kept by him in the sort of enclosed life which Flora knew from her days on the roof at Kasur. It is this incident which supplies material for a really close comparison between the writing of Flora Annie Steel and that of Rudyard Kipling.

Two of Kipling's most remarkable stories are directly concerned with such a situation. *Beyond the Pale*, perhaps the more famous of the two, describes a love affair between an Englishman and an Indian girl, an affair carried on secretly by way of a window on a back alley. The romance has begun when the Englishman hears Bisea, laugh and serenades her with a verse from what Kipling has called the *Love Song of Hyar Dyal*.

Now in his eighties, the Argentinian writer, Jorges Luis Borges has lost none of his admiration for Kipling's works, nor any of his wide knowledge of their content. Borges' failed eyesight has made him dependent on others to read Kipling's stories to him, but the *Love Song of Hyar Dyal* he can still quote from memory. To a recent visitor Borges explained that this was a legacy from his father, who was in the habit of reciting the verses which play a vital part in *Beyond the Pale*.

Bisea, the Indian widow, sends a message of invitation to Trejago, the Englishman. She greets him from the darkness above with this invocation:

"Alone upon the housetops, to the North.
I turn and watch the lightning in the sky,
The glamour of thy footsteps in the North,
Come back to me, Beloved, or I die!"

The poetry which celebrates the love affair has crossed continents oceans and years to find a home in the memory of another great poet, but in fact the affair wrecks itself because it is a liaison between East and West.

The tragic climax comes as a result of a lover's quarrel over the little more than ordinary civility of Trejago to a fellow countrywoman. Little Bisea cries in anguished passion that she knows she is unworthy of her lover. "I am only a black girl and the widow of a black man". These phrases are an exaggeration of despair, for she has "little feet like marigolds", being "fairer than bar-gold in the Mint".

After giving his mistress time to grow cooler, Trejago, craving her company, returns to the window in the dark alley. Bisea can only

84

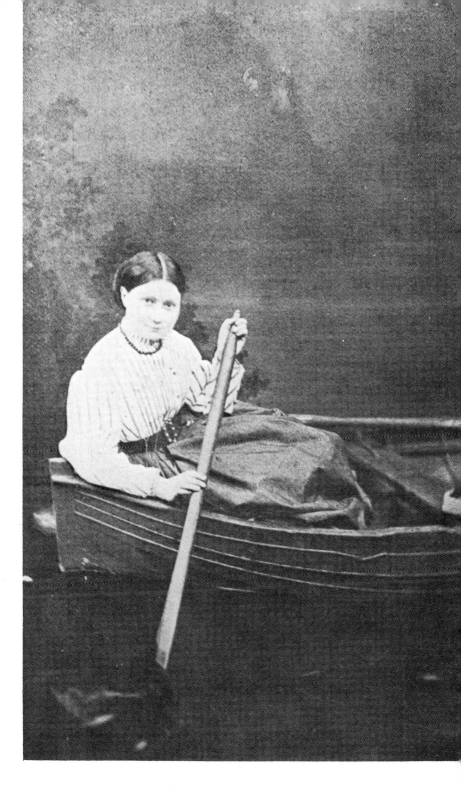

Flora Annie Webster in 1867

Bazaar at Kasauli

University of the Punjab. Foundation Stone Ceremony, Lahore 1886,
performed by the Viceroy, Lord Dufferin

Lieutenant-Governor's Camp at Lahore

Commissioner's barge, Kashmir

Lahore Railway Station

Illustration by J. Lockwood Kipling from *Tales of the Punjab*, Macmillan 1894

Laurence Hope, author of *Indian Love Lyrics*. From a photograph by G. C. Beresford, London

Lahore Gate, Red Fort, Delhi

Rooftops at Lahore

Flora Annie Steel in 1897

William Heinemann *c.* 1913

Flora Annie Steel in the Garden of Fidelity at Talgarth with Angelo

Court of Hill, Shropshire

Flora Annie Steel in later life

stretch out her arms to him, her hands having been cut off at the wrists. Her lover is attacked and wounded by an unseen avenger of the family's honour, but he escapes alive, never to know what has caused the horrible retribution. The window on the alley is blocked up. Among the maze of houses there is no way of knowing what might be the front door of Bisea's home. Impenetrable, the city jungle symbolizes a world where love is forbidden to cross the frontiers of race.

Even more moving, and closer to Flora's handling of the theme, is Kipling's story *Without Benefit of Clergy*. Like Jim Douglas, Flora's hero, Kipling's Englishman, in this case an Indian Civilian, has bought a girl, setting her up as his mistress, with her mother as bawd turned housekeeper. From this mercenary transaction has grown a love that shines like the stars which Holden and Ameera watch from their roof top. Sent away on a spell of duty, the Englishman awaits the birth of their child in desperate anxiety, all the more intense from the need to keep his expectation secret. When the son is born the delight they share is without thought for the future. At the child's death the mother's distraction is almost suicidal in its frenzy.

The rains are delayed, while cholera invades the city. Forebodingly, a medical officer prophesies that Nature is going to audit her accounts with a big red pencil. Ameera is among those struck out, dying just before the monsoon breaks. The rains bring relief to the stricken city, but wash away the house that has held so much love and so much pain.

There has been argument as to whether Kipling was himself emotionally involved in such a love affair, but certainly he must have come across similar situations on which his imagination could build. Much of the force of the story comes from the contrast between the delicacy of the hidden romance and the insensitive chaff of Holden's colleagues at his club. Incidentally, one of these, a Deputy Commissioner, has come in from his district to take advantage of a scheme for famine relief works. If he can pre-empt his share, he will be supplied with labour to finish a canal, a pet project for which he has been striving for many months. The real world of Henry Steel, whose policy of planting needed above all reliable irrigation, has come very close to the fiction of Rudyard Kipling.

Both Kipling's stories had appeared before *On the Face of the Waters* was published, even before Flora had returned to Delhi for her research into the Mutiny archives. It is unlikely that she had not read the stories, or at least heard them discussed, but she handled what was basically the same situation in a manner all her own. An acute touch on the part of the author reveals Douglas as having bought Zora to make his own life more agreeable. Seen as an outcast by his compatriots, he has no such need to keep his domestic arrangements secret, a necessity that tormented Ameera's lover. On the other hand Douglas lacks the passion of Holden, who could rejoice with Ameera at the birth of their son and grieve sincerely with her at the child's death.

Douglas, in his heart, is even conscious of a shameful feeling of relief when Zora's child is born dead. He accepts Zora's worship, but, wearied of India, he hears the Highlands calling. Ameera, in *Without Benefit of Clergy*, is jealous that her youth will pass more quickly than that of the *memsahibs*, showing a pathetic realism which her lover silences with kisses. In a reversed situation, Jim Douglas is the realist. His Indian mistress is as pale as a moonbeam, but he still shrinks from the idea of fathering an Eurasian child, knowing the perplexities that mixed blood would bring with it.

Zora is fading in the pavilion of love, where she awaits Douglas' visits as her only interest or pleasure. The house is kept by Tara-Devi, a widow, beautiful but living what may be called a posthumous life. She is the twin sister of Soma, formerly soldier servant to Douglas. By what she considers a disastrous misfortune, Soma had aroused Douglas' interest in the funeral of Soma's brother-in-law. Finding the widow about to cast herself onto the funeral pyre, Douglas has interfered to prevent her immolation. Tara has ambivalent feelings towards her rescuer.

It is here that, according to Mrs Patwardhan, the confusion between two forms of *suttee* occurs. Consequently Tara's continual wail, that she is *suttee* and may yet join her husband by fire, is a novelist's strategem rather than a correct religious attitude. Having failed to die with her husband on his funeral pyre, Tara would not expect to join him by a later burning, which is the fate that Flora eventually metes out to the death-obsessed widow. Uncompromising in its staunchness, Tara's character seems to have something in common with that of Fazli, the mysterious but devoted *ayah* of Flora's daughter Mabel.

Having agreed not to expose Major Erlton's trickery on the race course, Douglas finds himself to be near bankruptcy. Looking for employment, he seeks an interview with a Civilian high up in the Political Department. Paradoxically, the kind of spy work which Douglas is prepared to take on is a first step towards casting off his alter ego, Greyman. Needing a safe conduct before he slips into the native world, he asks for it to be made out in his real name.

Douglas's interview with the civilian official is monitored by what Flora calls a military magnate. While allowing both men the qualities of brains and courage, Flora gets a few side swipes in at their unwillingness to accept opinions or information that do not agree with their own fixed ideas. The interview itself is fraught with signs of future trouble. Particularly ominous is the rumour, reported by Douglas, that sacks of flour, supplied to the sepoy soldiers are said to have had ground bone as an ingredient.

This piece of malicious propaganda, as well as threatening to undermine the loyalty of the sepoys, also introduces an element of clowning into the novel, bubbling up as a kind of Shakespearean light relief. Jhungi/Bhungi, an interchangeable pair of brothers, possibly in reality one man, are liable to appear phantomlike, evaporating in the same way. Douglas relies on this contact to keep him informed about what Kipling, in this connection, called "the drift of the undercurrents". It is when Douglas himself is drifting, disguised through the Fair of the Festival of Spring that he has his first experience of the spirit which animates Alice Gissing.

Gissing, her husband, is a contractor, supplying beer to the troops. On his profits he is able to live in a nabob style already out of date. His hospitality, Flora wrote, was of the sort that made few concessions to climate, sending premiums required for life insurance in India, in byegone days, up to the equivalent of war rates. As Alice Gissing sits at the head of her husband's table, the innocence of her white muslin and blue ribbons is emphasized by the delicacy with which she dips her lips into a foam-covered glass of porter.

After luncheon, Major Erlton in attendance, Alice is driven to the cemetery where her infant daughter, child of an earlier marriage to a handsome Eurasian, is buried. The flowers she places on the grave have been made into a tight bunch by the gardener, a hard-wearing bouquet designed to last a week. Mrs Erlton, while rejecting her own transplanting to India, struggles to cultivate a garden for which the highest compliment is to exclaim at its Englishness. From among his wife's carefully nurtured pansies Major Erlton takes a handful in an attempt to join in the weekly rite at the tomb of his mistress' child. He is met with good-tempered disapproval of such an ephemeral offering, which will perish immediately in the unrelenting Indian heat.

Leaving the cemetery, Alice wishes to see the Fair, the Festival of Spring, but on the way an Indian child is run over by Erlton's dog-cart. The child has made a sudden dash into the road and, though the shafts of the dog cart snap from the strain when Erlton reins in the mare, the accident cannot be prevented. Mastering the shock of horror, Alice, essentially tough, analyses the situation. Neither race, she says, can regard such an accident to the other except with detachment. From experience of the Indian point of view Alice knows that to her family the child was only an expendable girl. Compensation, readily accepted, will heal the immediate grief, one less mouth to feed and rupees for those remaining, which includes the boy-child whose loss would have caused infinitely more wailing.

Alice has been given a lift from the scene of the accident by a man who has just announced that he will be telling his wife that she must, in future, cut Mrs Gissing. Well aware of his embarrassment, Alice conveys her knowledge to her disapproving rescuer. She then relieves him of her compromising presence by transferring herself to the buggy of her newest, still illusioned admirer, young Mainwaring, who is ordered to drive her to the Fair. He, bewitched and unable to protest at whims he is too naive to understand, can only follow Alice on foot into a crowd which is laughing licentiously at a side-show. Laughing herself, she asks the audience to let her through, continuing to laugh when she realizes that their obligingness in moving aside comes from a malicious desire to humiliate an arrogant *memsahib*.

"Two white-masked figures, clasped waist to waist, were waltzing tipsily. One had a curled flaxen wig, a muslin dress distended by an all too visible crinoline giving full play to a pair of prancing brown legs. The other wore an old staff uniform, cocked hat and feather complete. The flaxen curls rested on the tarnished epaulette, the unembracing arms flourished brandy bottles.

"It was a vile travesty; and the Englishwoman turned instinctively to the Englishman as if doubtful what to do, how to take it; but the passion on his boyish face seemed to make things clear—to give her the clue, and she gripped his hand hard. 'Don't be a fool!' she whispered fiercely. 'Laugh! It's the only thing to do.' Her own rang out shrill above the uncertain stir in the crowd, taken aback in its merriment.

"But something else rose above it also. A single word—
'Bravo!'"

Excited by this applause of her sang-froid, Alice deduces that it must have come from a man she has noticed in the crowd, a man fairer than his fellows and wearing the fur cap of the Pathan. Her deduction is correct. The cry of 'Bravo!' has come from Douglas showing him to be a poor hand at disguise where his emotions are concerned.

Douglas, does, however, soon get an opportunity to improve his technique. Actually he is aware that his disguise is far from convincing, even his walk being in itself a betrayal. With nothing to lose, he pursues the masked dancers into their booth, intending to assert by a beating that British officers and their women are not to be mocked with impunity. He suspects that the dancers have been Bungi/Jhungi, adepts at serving two or more masters.

It is no surprise to find that the guilty brother has fled, leaving the innocent one of the pair to explain and exploit the situation. Also seated in the booth is Tiddu, of the tribe of many faces. This chameleon of an impersonator offers Douglas his help in the matter of disguise, at a price to be agreed. After a demonstration of Tiddu's effortless changes of personality and sex, Douglas sees that here is an ideal instructor for undercover work. As Flora says, the infinitely subtle differences of language and accent in India make an outsider's speech the factor most likely to betray his alien origins. Bearing this in mind, she ends the first book of the novel with Douglas posing as a deaf and dumb driver of a bullock. The disguise has been supplied by Tiddu, expert in such matters. It is a comic touch that the bullock should be carrying the paraphernalia of the mocking show that outraged Douglas's British sensibilities. As he drives the bullock forward in the cool breeze that blows just before dawn, the morning gun booms out and the English flag rises above the city of Lucknow.

With the opening of the second book of *On the Face of the Waters*, Flora moves her story not only to Delhi, but into the Palace where the last of the Mughals is living in a drug-induced dream of past greatness. From this remains of an Empire, the Prime Minister and Chief Eunuch is carried forth in a palanquin. Delayed by the slow recital of the keeper of the daily record, he curses the trembling official in a scene which has a *brio* comparable to the auctioning of the King of Oudh's menagerie.

Up till the appearance of the Chief Eunuch, the twin brother and sister, Soma and Tara, have been the principal Indian figures in the novel. On moving the scene to Delhi, Flora adds a flood of new characters to her cast. Confidently, she describes the intrigues that surround the King of Delhi and Zeenut Maihl, the last of his favourite wives, who keeps her influence by cozening the King that he may still be able to father a child by her. The King himself gives his audiences in the Diwan-i-Khas where is inscribed the triple affirmation, "If there is a paradise on earth it is here, it is here, it is here." These words, in the most beautiful of Persian script, are true of the Hall of Private Audience even to this day, though in the time of the

89

last Mughal its frequenters were apt to resemble emissaries from hell rather than messengers from paradise.

Although her predeliction seems to have been for men who smelt of the open air as opposed to the musk popular among Mughals, Flora shows signs of having fallen in love with her interpretation of the character of Mirza Abool Bukr. Dashing, a frequenter of the city's brothels, given to swaying drunkenly while he sings lewd songs, Abool Bukr is partly redeemed by an insinuating charm. He is also restrained by the influence of a high-minded kinswoman, who shuns the claustrophobic Palace to live austerely in the city.

Only slightly older than her nephew by marriage, Princess Fark-hoonda Zamani, called Newasi, allows no indecorum in her relation-ship with Abool Bukr. Son of the last direct heir of the King, the Prince is reasonably sure of his inheritance if he can outlast a series of uncles. In the meantime his most innocent occupation is to sing the songs of Hafiz, Sa'adi and Omar Khayyám to Newasi, who does her best to raise him above a state of increasing decadence.

These are historical characters, from now on the novel being increasingly concerned with events that actually happened. Jim Douglas, the Erltons, Alice Gissing, Tara and Soma, meet Indians and British of whose lives and deaths there is much documentation. Above all their fates are influenced by the character of John Nichol-son, who fell leading the attack on the Lahore Gate of Delhi. If Flora was fascinated by Abool Bukr, she had a hero worship for Nicholson equal to that of his Multani Horsemen. These regarded their duty to be to Nicholson alone, retreating to the hills when their leader was dead and their desire for loot satisfied.

In the last days before the Mutiny there was a circulation of *chupattis* from village to village in the Punjab, a movement whose origins and meaning has never, it seems, been fully explained. A runner would appear with a cake of the unleavened bread, bearing also the message that two more were to be baked and sent in specified directions. The message might be said to have been its own meaning. The fear of breaking the chain, re-inforced by a memory that long ago *chupattis* had travelled through the country-side as portents of some looming disaster, kept the cakes moving, a manifestation of the breath that God was sending into the world. Flora paints a convinc-ing picture of a village receiving and passing on these symbols, no-one fully understanding what they portend.

There are a few minor points of military detail about which, Flora wrote, she had been detected in error. Otherwise her grasp of the events of the siege of Delhi, both within and without the city, has been generally agreed to be masterly. Within this framework she works out the crisis in the relationship of Major Erlton and Alice Gissing. The latter, undeniably the most interesting of the novel's characters, finds herself to be pregnant. Struggling to act to a higher standard than he usually maintains, Erlton writes to his wife, asking her if she will divorce him.

Although the situation is tragic, Erlton's letter is one of the comic highlights of the novel. As he puts it to himself, his wife has been only too apt to make him feel a fool or a beast. Kate's deflating attitude inhibits her husband, as a letter writer, from making his meaning clear.

Erlton writes that "circumstances over which we had no control (he felt rather proud of this circumlocution for a circumstance due entirely to his own volition) make it necessary for me to leave you." He goes on to say that he wishes to marry Alice Gissing when it is possible to do so. He mentions, in passing, that Gissing may make trouble, adultery being a criminal offence in India. Kate, he feels, will hardly care, but he has regrets about their boy. Erlton adds enigmatically that at least the child is a boy and the other may not be.

By her own account, Flora had had considerable experience of matrimonial upsets among her acquaintances. She turned this experience to good use in the confrontation between Kate Erlton, steely in her determination not to release her unloved husband, and Alice Gissing, whose clear blue eyes see the characters of all concerned without any veil of sentiment. It becomes apparent that Kate has failed to understand the implications of her husband's letter, so an appeal that Alice should consider a mother's feelings misfires. Typically, Alice finds her lover's failure to make his meaning explicit absurd but just what might be expected from any man.

At the climax of the scene, when Kate is dizzy from the effort to take in the fact of Alice's pregnancy, history intervenes. A neighbour's child, Sonny Seymour, is seen to be in acute danger. Trailing the chain of a cockatoo behind him, Sonny is running away from a fanatical Muslim who, lance in hand, is intent on retrieving the bird. It is the same bird whose cry of the Faith, "Deen! Deen! Futteh Mahomed!" was heard in the first pages of the book.

Alice, who has just had news of the killings in Delhi, rushes to the rescue of Sonny, which she accomplishes by deflecting the attack onto herself, a delicate figure in a frilly peignoir. At this moment Jim Douglas arrives. By a complication of the plot, he has found himself obliged to promise Erlton that he will rescue Alice from her perilously situated house. Douglas shoots the attacker, but not before a mortal wound has been inflicted on Alice. This is a private disaster. On the wider stage mutiny has broken out at Meerut, the sepoys having then marched on Delhi.

Twice before Douglas has had cause to admire Alice's courage; once when she laughed at the ribald dancers, and once, in camp, when he has grabbed her in his arms on seeing an apparently lifeless branch make a serpentine movement. Now when he holds her in his arms again, her dying words are a laughing question, why does he not say "bravo"? Douglas seems prone to necrophilic situations. For the second time in the novel he holds a beautiful dead woman in his arms. He had mourned for Zora, if with reservations, but for Alice, barely known to him, there is a stronger pang of regret. Her reckless courage had found its response in his own nature.

The end of Alice is also the end of her still illusioned admirer, young Mainwaring. In a frenzy that causes Indians to shun him as possessed of the devil, he fights his way to Alice's house. Finding her dead, he lays her out in his uniform coat, before collapsing from his wounds. Mainwaring possesses Alice more completely in death than he ever did in life.

If the sudden cutting off of Alice's life dissolves the crisis between the Erltons, it also causes a lessening of tension among the English characters. Kate, with her piety and her insularity, has, perhaps unfairly, failed to win much of the reader's sympathy. She has been seen to make no surrender to her surroundings, keeping her home as an island of Englishness. Her ignorance of the vernacular is so complete that she can correct a pattern for her tailor without noticing that it is cut from a paper proclamation which asserts that "The Sword is the Key of Heaven".

This insularity now gives way to the need to survive. Kate must be concealed in the city of Delhi, in the midst of enemies vowed to achieve the Key of Heaven by the slaughter of the Infidel. Tara, her feelings for Douglas still ambiguous, acts both as a servant and an initiator into Indian ways, so that Kate may not be detected as an Englishwoman. Finally Kate escapes back to the Ridge, where the besiegers of Delhi are established. Her adventures are a mixture of passivity and the need for sudden desperate action.

The little boy, Sonny, has also to be passed off as an Indian child. Somehow, between Tara, Tiddu of the many-faced tribe, and Douglas himself, three separate escapes are accomplished. At a perilous moment in her own adventure, Kate finds herself obliged to throw herself on the mercy of Newasi. She will otherwise be the victim of Abool Bakr, sworn killer of infidels. Newasi does protect

Kate, but at the cost of an estrangement from the Prince. This is a device of Flora's to explain the removal of the last restraint that Newasi exercised over her nephew. Without her influence he advances along a reckless road which is to lead him to death in the dust outside Humayun's Tomb.

Major Erlton has arrived among the besiegers of Delhi, where he is seen to be behaving with nonchalant courage. When Kate, who finally escapes along the river, arrives at the British lines, her husband is there to welcome her, but he naturally feels that their situation is one that cannot be left unresolved. It seems that he resolves it by a bullet behind his ear, though this is a last secret shared by him and Kate.

Flora's admiration for John Nicholson brings this General frequently into the action of the story. It is Nicholson who tells Kate that Erlton's name has gone forward for the Victoria Cross. At the same time he urges her to make what recompense she can to Douglas for the dangers run on her behalf. Erlton's tactful exit makes it possible for the reward to be Kate herself. Nicholson, as has been said, is mortally wounded in the attack on Delhi. The last of the Mughals goes into captivity and exile. Tara makes her final sacrifice by fetching Kate to Douglas's sickbed, then casting herself into the flames that are devouring her former home. Even if this episode is ceremonially incorrect it makes, combined with the capture of Delhi, a high flourish with which *On the Face of the Waters* ends.

Such a summary as the above is highly selective, omitting a number of sub-plots and historical incidents which Flora skilfully wove together. To give only one example, Douglas sends a telegram, refusing further under-cover work. He happens to see a telegram from Erlton summoning Alice Gissing to join him at Meerut, where the powder keg of the Mutiny is about to explode. These telegrams are part of a melodramatic situation. Flora, however, brings in the reality of the historic moment by quoting the only message of alarm that was sent on the night of May 10th 1857.

Flora describes this as the strangest telegram that ever came as sole warning to an Empire that its very foundation was being attacked. The telegram was sent from Meerut to Agra by the postmaster's niece. It ran as follows: "The Cavalry have risen, setting fire to their own houses, besides having killed and wounded all European officers and soldiers they could find near the lines. If Aunt intends starting to-morrow, please detain her, as the van has been prevented from leaving the station." Among the many agonizing confusions of the time the niece of the postmaster of Meerut appears to have had a remarkably firm grasp of the essence of the situation.

More than once Flora showed a fondness for speculating on what would happen after the end of a novel, when her characters had been left to their own devices. With her novel of the Mutiny she supplied two appendices. The first is the report of a Collector and Magistrate, such an officer as Henry Steel was to be in later days. Building up this composite report from her study of those preserved at Delhi, she included an anonymous but well-balanced statement of post-Mutiny morale. "It will take years for one race to regain its confidence, the other its self-respect."

The second appendix takes the form of a letter from a platonic admirer of Mrs Erlton, whose piety and frigidity seems not to have discouraged other men as it did her husband. The letter congratulates her on her approaching marriage to Jim Douglas, now conveniently become a Scottish landowner. The admirer, a soldier by then doing civil work, has also found himself somewhat baffled by a claim of Tiddu, of the tribe of many faces, on behalf of Jhungi, or possibly Bhungi. Doubt prevailing as to whether one, both or neither has been killed, it is unlikely that the matter will ever be regulated.

Before he died, John Nicholson told Mrs Erlton that her husband's name had gone forward for the Victoria Cross. The letter to Mrs Erlton includes a comment on the awarding of this decoration, an incident which Flora presumably knew to be true. Asked for a nomination to receive the Victoria Cross, the troopers of the 9th Lancers sent in the name of their regimental *bhisti* (water-carrier). Their selection was challenged as unsuitable, but the troopers refused to amend it, on the grounds that, if he did not get it, no one else deserved it. No one can have been less surprised than Flora to learn that Government then chose not to make the award to anyone in the 9th Lancers. This story might well be the germ of Kipling's poem *Gunga Din*; in which case the *bhisti* has had enduring fame greater than any decoration could bestow.

The celebrity which came to Flora with the success of *On the Face of the Waters* filled her with unselfconscious pleasure. She accepted praise for the fidelity of her Indian background, her interpretation of Indian character and her grasp of military history, with the knowledge that it was the not unmerited acclaim of hard work and sympathy for her subject. One tribute in particular gave her the satisfaction of feeling that she had written more than a sensational novel about terrible events. An unknown correspondent, who must have been at least in his sixties, wrote to say that his wife had died in the Mutiny. After forty years, he told Flora, her book had at last enabled him to forgive India.

XII

Suddenly a Lioness

When Flora had finished *On the Face of the Waters*, she knew that she had worked to a high standard. Some pages she had written as often as fifteen times, until she herself was satisfied. She had, of course, the advantage of writing of a period familiar to every reader of English novels. Mrs Patwardhan has calculated that at least six novels had already been published with the Mutiny as their main theme. One of these that can conveniently be compared with Flora's masterpiece being actually published in the same year. Its title was *Flotsam*, its author Henry Seton Merriman.

Nowadays the name of Henry Seton Merriman is rarely heard, but his novels of adventure, mainly historical and set in foreign parts, were once immensely popular. Possibly his tall, fair, consistently moral heroes and heroines eventually proved too smooth for readers accustomed to deeper psychological probings. On the other hand, his portraits of Carlist rebels, agents of foreign powers and wise old priests, usually French or Spanish, were lively, and he had a nice line in crooked business men. This side of his writing has had an undeniable influence on a later generation of adventure stories. Dynasties may have been toppled, aristocracies ruined, but agents of foreign powers, as employed by Merriman, still remain to supply an element of sinister romance in a drab world.

Merriman took the view that, to quote a phrase of Flora's, the Mutiny was the Epic of the Race. He concentrated on one young British soldier, whose career went downhill in a series of financial and marital disasters. He lacked both Flora's first-hand experience of Indian life and her sympathy for raffish types such as Alice Gissing and Major Erlton. Merriman's heroes and villains are kept firmly within their moulds. Of the few Indians who play a part in *Flotsam*,

95

one turns out to be an Englishman in disguise, but without the experience of native life that makes Douglas's changes of dress convincing.

The Fall of Delhi, with the temptation to loot, is only another step in the downfall of a man who might have been a hero had he not become *Flotsam*. The Siege and Fall of Delhi is at the centre of Merriman's novel, but it had been used by writers for their purposes long before Merriman's day. As early as the 1860's, Charlotte M. Yonge was already employing the theme as material to further the plots of her stories, with the confidence that her readers would understand its relevance.

With some literary success behind her, it was reasonable of Flora to expect that Macmillan, publisher of her previous novel, would welcome *On the Face of the Waters*. She herself respected the firm, a respect which had survived its reader's criticism of *Red Rowans*. This criticism had praised her knowledge of London, where she had never lived, but condemned her for ignorance of the West Highlands, her girlhood's holiday home. With Kipling in their stable, Macmillan was no stranger to realism in writing of Indian matters, but nevertheless they rejected *On the Face of the Waters*.

This unexpected slap in the face did distress Flora for a period, particularly as her respected publisher seems to have suggested that the book was weak in its writing. The hobgoblin which leads publishers to reject a book that becomes a rival's best-seller often prompts them to do so from assumptions that prove to be fallacious. Apart from any weakness in the writing, Macmillan's may have felt that the Epic of the Race was too deeply revered for the public to be sympathetic towards a book in which the faults on both sides were so clearly set out.

Never for long put out of countenance, Flora set herself to show her faith in her own work. She also had the good fortune to have another publisher up her sleeve with whom she was to enjoy a happy business friendship. The earliest contact with her new publisher dated back to Flora's first book, *Wide Awake Stories*. It has been mentioned that she had preferred the first Indian edition of this collection of folk-lore to the grander English edition retitled *Tales of the Punjab*. Although unattractively produced, the Indian edition was also to have an important influence on Flora's career. Published in Bombay in 1884, under the imprint of the Education Society's Press, the title page of *Wide-Awake Stories* also bore the words London: Trübner & Co., a firm which at that date employed a young man called William Heinemann, ambitiously intent on learning the business

Although only twenty-one years old William Heinemann, son of a naturalized German father, was already determined to set up on his own account in publishing. He regarded Trübner's office as the spring-board from which he would acquire the business impetus to launch himself. Seldom has a young man's plan to enter publishing met with more abounding success. At the age of twenty-seven, Heinemann started his own publishing house, equipped with the technical knowledge he had gained in his apprenticeship at Trübner's. This expertise was arguably almost more valuable than his enthusiastic interest in literature.

Besides Heinemann himself, the firm at its beginning in Bedford Street, Covent Garden, was run by one clerk and one office boy. As the business flourished and expanded, however, its founder seems to have felt the need for a balance to his own mercurial temperament. Searching for this, he enlisted as a partner Sydney Pawling, who had worked in the solid, if unstimulating House of Mudie. Pawling was, it appears, almost a caricature of a sporting Englishman, the antithesis of the cosmopolitan Heinemann. This combination of opposites, as it might be egg-yolk and oil, made an excellent mayonnaise, though the partners took some trouble to conceal the fact. According to the unreliable evidence of Ford Madox Ford, Pawling would let out an anguished cry of "It's not cricket," when Heinemann had been beguiled into making an unwarrantably large advance to the chronically hard-up Joseph Conrad.

Frederic Whyte's biography of William Heinemann appeared in the year before Flora's death. Whyte gave it as his opinion that she was the author whose books afforded Heinemann himself the most pleasure in publishing. Asked for her reminiscences by Mr Whyte, Mrs Steel replied with gusto undiminished by age. Sydney Pawling she described as a connection of her family who had invited her to a dinner party. William Heinemann took her down to dinner, an immediate *rapport* being established. He would certainly have known her name from his days with Trübner and, whatever her commitments to Macmillan, he at once recognized her as a woman of unusual gifts who would be an acquisition to any discriminating publisher.

Some authors recollected that one way in which the partners balanced each other was to excuse reluctance to oblige in business matters by invoking the disapproval of Pawling or Heinemann as the case might be. Flora, connected with Pawling, could by-pass this difficulty. Additionally, by becoming a best-seller, she vindicated Heinemann's judgement that *On the Face of the Waters* could not be better done. When the book hit the jackpot excited telegrams came flashing to Flora from her publisher, but besides this business success their personal sympathy increased. This included Heinemann's love of good living. Flora considered him to be a true *gourmet*. She devoted careful attention to providing him with *sole au vin blanc* for which he had the highest standard. Even a visit to the Steels' Highland home was made delightful to a man indifferent to sport by the dish of *perdrix aux choux* which greeted him on arrival.

To return to the publishing history of *On the Face of the Waters*, its author was able to record that, thirty-three years after its publication, the book had never been out of print and was still selling. The question of its original sale to the United States had brought out the best of Flora's crusading zeal. She refused to accept a royalty of ten per cent on the novel, which, at that date, was all that American publishers were prepared to offer. Sticking out for twelve per cent, she knew that she was campaigning for others less able than herself to insist on a just percentage.

In answer to her agent's appeal that she should accept the lower rate, thereby avoiding piratical publication, she sent orders that the book should be published at her own expense. The £400 that it would cost her she was prepared to hazard. Flora thought the money would be well spent if it improved the lot of British writers unable, from scanty means, to fight for themselves. Immediately offers poured in, on her terms, from publishers whose bluff had been called. It is pleasant to know that the publisher who eventually won the auction had the grace to repay the £400 which Flora had so gallantly risked.

Success in sales was equalled by praise from reviewers, with the inevitable comparisons with Kipling. In the previous chapter the separate approach to the same theme of Flora Annie Steel and Rudyard Kipling has been discussed. Even more in contrast is the literary style in which the theme—love affairs between Englishmen and Indian girls—is handled. Kipling was eighteen years the younger. He had, in his boyhood, come into contact with an artistic life where memories of revolt and experiment were still alive. Additionally Kipling had been through a gruelling course of journalistic training. As a result even his philosophical reflections are a means by which the reader learns more about the characters of a story and their particular situation.

Flora, on the other hand, belongs essentially to an earlier literary tradition. She spreads her canvas with an enthusiasm that carries the reader along with her, exhilarated by the tacking and going about.

There is, however, a reef on which both Flora Annie Steel and Rudyard Kipling come to grief. This reef is the convention that children should talk in a lisping manner, uttering quaint thoughts, to be received by their elders with a kindly smile that is also a tribute to clear-eyed childhood.

In fairness to Kipling, by the time he came to write *Puck of Pook's Hill* he had changed his technique, but there is a hair-curling quality of embarrassment in the lisping children of his earlier stories. Flora's children are even more exaggerated in their artlessness. At times it is hard to believe that she had grown up among an intellectually lively tribe of brothers and sisters, or that she had any recollection as to what it was like to think a child's thoughts and put them into words.

Kipling and Flora cannot be entirely blamed for conforming to what was an accepted literary convention of the late Victorian period. Earlier there had been less archness and more realism when such writers as Charlotte M. Yonge or Juliana Horatia Ewing brilliantly evoked the moods of childhood. It is unimaginable that either of these writers would have put into the mouth of Kipling's Wee Willie Winkie the query "Are you fond of vis big girl, Coppy?" Or permitted Flora's Sonny Seymour to wail, "Sonny's always flightened wizout hith muvver."

Perhaps from increased objectivity, Kipling's and Flora's portraits of Indian children are much less distorted by quaintness. Little Tobrah, who in the interests of his own survival, has remorselessly pushed his sister down a well, is perhaps exceptionally free from sentimentality, but he is also completely believable. Flora's description of the querulous dying Sa'adut, a little prince but the Heir of Nothingness, makes the English boy, son of the Lieutenant-Governor in *Voices in the Night*, appear dull, not to say stodgy.

The success of *On the Face of the Waters* turned its author into a lioness, a transformation which encouraged the Steels to establish a temporary base in London. This experiment coincided with Queen Victoria's Diamond Jubilee. Throughout the summer of 1897, London was packed for the celebrations, and the crowds included many who wished to make Flora's acquaintance. Her enjoyment was diluted by the feeling that she was sometimes handed round like a plate of cakes at a tea party. It was certainly excusable to feel some annoyance when a lady, unable to approach the lioness more closely, called over the intervening heads: "Thanks! I have just been reading your splendid *On the Surface of the Sea*."

Infinitely more satisfying was her meeting with George White, her old friend from her early days in Dalhousie. He was now

Commander-in-Chief, an eminence in his profession which, added to his Victoria Cross, was to earn him a statue in Portland Place. There he still gazes from his saddle towards what was once the Langham Hotel. His reunion with Flora took place at a big ball where decorations abounded. Spotting his old friend in the crowd, the Field Marshal, glittering with medals, hurried to greet the now famous author, both hands outstretched. "'You've done it too,' he said," charmingly equating their respective successes. Together they looked back to the days at the foot of Holy Himalaya, when he had seen himself as a soldier with no prospects. Flora's advice to persevere, which White might have disregarded, coming as it did from the anxiously pregnant wife of a young Indian Civilian, turned out to have been superlatively worth following.

Apart from being a Jubilee lioness, Flora organized a celebration on her own initiative. The Jubilee, she pointed out was to celebrate sixty years of rule by a woman, but the festivities were conducted mostly by and for males. In no way were women showing that they too could hold banquets compared to those promoted by men. Flora's idea, that one hundred and twenty women, each remarkable in her own sphere, should ask an equivalent male partner to a dinner, was a scheme taken up with enthusiasm. While implementing the plan tricky situations inevitably arose, but they were mostly so comic that they sent Flora into gales of laughter. A hostess who had graduated among the social complications of Kasur, had little to fear when faced by High Society in Diamond Jubilee Year.

Arthur Balfour, nephew of Lord Salisbury the Prime Minister and future Leader of the Conservative Party, was the most popular nominee, but Flora does not say how his person was distributed among the competing ladies. Neither does she give the name of the distinguished male involved in a current scandal. There was argument as to whether the lady linked with him should not be banned from the dinner, although her partner was a guest to be desired on account of his public position. Flora carried the day by persuading the committee to accept her precept that it would be impertinent for such a body to censure, by implication, what was indisputably a family affair.

Moral dilemmas did not prevent the dinner from being a dazzling success. A bower was created at the Grafton Galleries, a background for a gourmet's banquet, produced, under Flora's direction, by M. Benoist of Piccadilly. Such commonplaces as turtle soup and duckling with green peas were barred from the menu, though Flora did not say by what delicacies they were replaced. As the double tickets

100

were only £2.5s with wine, the evening was not only a social tour de force but a gastronomic bargain.

There is evidence that Flora's feeling of responsibility towards the problems of India was not overlaid by the excitement of Jubilee Year. More than one letter from Flora Annie Steel appeared in *The Times*, the first being written from Aberdeenshire in the January of 1897. This was an appeal for orders for the gold thread workers of Delhi, reduced to sorry straits by a declaration of a "Sangat" by the priests of the Hindus, which banned giving in marriage with its ritual garments, for thirteen months. The gold thread workers were, Flora wrote, mostly respectable women, many of them members of the late Royal Family of Delhi. Another market, sales to visitors, had shrunk because of an outbreak of plague in Bombay. Flora's appeal was carefully phrased to attract buyers of varying means. Its success was immediate. She was able to write in May to thank the buyers, whose response had already enabled her to send £500 to the embroidresses.

The Steels had now moved to 29 Palace Gate, from whence Flora could try her paces as a lioness. She was therefore in a position to offer samples to show to would-be purchasers. Her most successful line seems to have been what she called Jubilee scarves, strips of muslin edged with gold thread. These sold at two shillings each, for the profit of the aged pensioners behind the curtains who had often figured in her books. Always a strong believer in the power of the subconscious over practical matters, Flora was struck by the way the sales graph sagged in a week when her own mind was preoccupied. With the return not of her attention, which had not slackened, but of her thoughts, the business of this clever cashing-in on Imperial enthusiasm once more boomed.

A darker aspect of life in the sub-continent had obtruded itself during the summer session of Parliament, when the House of Lords had debated the shocking increase in venereal disease among the British Army in India. The tone of the debate, the speakers including the Archbishop of Canterbury, was sensible and humane, contrary to later beliefs that Victorians were averse to facing sexual problems. Flora's opinion on the subject has been mentioned earlier, a protest at the regulations which hindered both the inspection of women and making precautions against contagion available to the soldiers. This opinion seems to have been shared by most of the peers who spoke on the subject of the health of the Army in India, agreeing that, with young men kept in barracks all day and then released into the temptations of the night, trouble could only be expected.

Whether or not she was gratified by the attitude of the House of Lords, Flora took exception to the behaviour of the new Lieutenant-Governor of the Punjab, Sir William Mackworth Young. It seems that he had put forward proposals for the examination of bazaar women which, in Flora's view, was asking for trouble of a different kind. She wrote once again to *The Times* in August 1897, her letter being printed in a rather obscure corner, whether because the subject was cold news or too indelicate for the main letter columns it is hard to say. Flora wrote that she would leave medical aspects to the medical profession, but she knew Sir William Mackworth Young personally and felt him to be behaving injudiciously. On the question of the examination of women it seemed to her that the prejudice aroused would be likely to follow the pattern of misapprehension which led to the tragedy of the Mutiny. It was to Flora both tragic and absurd that after forty years there should be the same uncomprehending lack of sympathy shown for the beliefs and prejudices of the Eastern mind.

With the object of collecting background material for the novel which was to be called *Voices in the Night*, Flora set sail in 1897 for what was to be her final experience of India. Richard Gillies Hardy, the friend who had first urged her to write, had been appointed to the Commissionership of Lucknow. As his wife felt obliged to stay with her children in England, Hardy took with him the three Steels as a useful replacement. Flora wished to found her novel on contemporary Lucknow, but she was willing to spare time from her research to act as hostess and to be once again the *burra mem*. Henry Steel could enjoy the riding and racing. Although their daughter Mabel was of a serious turn of mind, her parents thought it desirable that she should at least be offered a sample of social life in a military station.

Compared with Delhi, Flora found Lucknow to have an artificial character, socially and architecturally. This feeling may have come from her own approach to the story of the city. At Delhi she had willed herself back into the past with all its glories and horrors. As readers of *On the Face of the Waters* will know she found the past, which was, after all, part of her own childhood, an area in which she could move with sympathy. To Flora, wishing to write of her own day, the past at Lucknow seemed almost sinister in its obtrusiveness. It was as if the wounds of forty years before had left scars that were psychological as well as spiritual. Even the plethora of barbers' shops and *parfumeries* was an uneasy reminder of the malignant barber of the last King of Oudh. The influence of this evil genius had led not only to Lucknow becoming a byword for vice and corruption, but ultimately to the King's deposition and the auctioning of his menagerie.

Although she had a deep respect for the mental powers of the Nettleship brothers and their circle, Flora recorded that it was at Lucknow that she encountered abstract thought in its purest form. When the 3rd Baron Rayleigh and his wife came to stay with the Commissioner, Flora, as their hostess, naturally laid herself out to entertain them. The New Year Fair, supposedly barred to Europeans but open to Mrs Steel's enterprise as that of Delhi had been to Mrs Gissing's, proved fascinating to the future winner of the Nobel Prize for Physics. Additionally, Flora hired the most skilful conjurer in Lucknow to display his art to the honoured guests. It was here that Lord Rayleigh, discoverer of argon, came into his own. Much taken by the complexity of a trick in which a piece of string was cunningly manipulated, he retreated from the show, to be seen by Flora sitting apart in motionless contemplation. On returning to the party he dummoxed the conjuror by a faultless performance of the trick. Asked how he had arrived at the solution, Lord Rayleigh replied, 'By gradual elimination of all impossibles.''

Coincident with Flora's last visit to India was the total eclipse which, in 1898, blackened the sun's face. The band of its totality, where alone the sun's corona is visible and the earth seems bathed in a deep blue shadow, passed some thirty miles from Benares. Flora, however, chose to content herself with the partial eclipse as it would be visible from the Holy City, putting the human spectacle of the Magh Mela before the astronomical rarity. Nearly three million people were expected to come to Benares to wash away their sins in the sacred Ganges at this especially propitious moment. As Flora had foreseen, the drama of the Magh Mela was both terrifying and uplifting. An Indian dawn has a uniquely luminous quality, nowhere more so than at Benares, dawn being the hour when the dead are brought down to the ghats to be consumed by fire and the living come to make their holy ablutions. For weeks before the eclipse a cloud of apprehension had hung over Hindustan. No one knew of what the expected phenomenon might be an omen. Similarly, before the Mutiny, no one had known what the *chupattis* passed to different points of the compass had portended.

From a river steamer, Flora watched as the greyness intensified, shadowing the gilded temples in front of which the faces of the packed crowd looked for they knew not what. Uneasiness that sudden panic might galvanize the multitudes into disastrous motion had led to a state of carefully concealed alertness among the police, a minute force in proportion to a crowd supposedly under their control.

On a plinth nearby Flora could see a young police officer, viewing the shadow that was creeping across the sun through a piece of smoked glass. As the shadow grew deeper even Flora's strong nerves were shaken by a sudden, ghostly flight of temple pigeons. Darkness increased, the police officer continuing to concentrate on his piece of smoked glass, his only words a reiterated, "Patience, patience." Then, at last, the greyness that had made the watching faces ghastly gave way to gradually increasing light. The faithful plunged into the waters of salvation, while the police officer, relaxing his controlled calm, asked the river steamer to give him a glass of beer.

Flora's final exit from India was hardly the sort of farewell she would have wished to take of the country where she had worked so hard and learnt so much. The vital part played by mosquitoes in conveying malaria was still not entirely understood. Flora risked sleeping without a mosquito net in the Commissioner's house at Lucknow with the result that she developed a high fever. An additional aggravation came from the illness incapacitating her on a visit to General and Mrs Nicolson at Mhow. Here Flora lay for a fortnight in bed, presumably in no state to criticize the indecorous gowns of the author of "Pale hands I loved beside the Shalimar." Mhow lies down country from Lucknow, more or less on the way to Bombay where her family eventually conveyed her. Recovery set in at sea, but even in her delirium Flora retained some of her medical acumen. The picture she drew of the beast which she felt to be rioting through her veins was a startling likeness of the malarial microbe.

It seems as if on her last visit Flora came nearest to understanding the spirit of the sub-continent which had fascinated and baffled her for twenty years. To soothe her fever—terai fever as it was then called—she was given hashish. The beatific haze it induced left Flora wondering if hashish might not account for the subliminal state of mind which allowed Indians to accept the marvels of modern science, while retaining a belief in fantasies which would seem absurd to European children.

XIII

Gathering the Sheaves

If her final exit from India had taken place in a hazy anti-climax softened by hashish, Flora carried with her a literary harvest that was to last her for the next thirty years. Whether she was writing about the Mughal Emperors or, as in *Voices in the Night*, about the problems of a marriage between East and West, her belief in the immemorial quality of Indian life gave her the confidence to adapt her own experience to either period. Often that self-confidence led her to draw conclusions opposed to those of her contemporaries. More than once, in *The Garden of Fidelity*, she expressed her conviction that, until purdah was abandoned by all classes, Indian women would remain in the state of subjugation recorded in the Artha Sastra, a writing dating from the 3rd century B.C.

Of purdah itself Flora's opinion contradicted the theory that it was a custom imposed by Muslim invaders, because it occurred in its strictest form in areas outside Mahomedan influence. She saw it as a logical result of the attitude that women existed to bear sons. Seclusion was therefore essential to ensure that the paternity of sons could not be doubted. Questions of support, comfort or affection were all secondary to this consideration. Familiar as she was with the delicious intrigues arising from an enclosed life, even acknowledging that its inhabitants often valued the zenana as a symbol of gentility, Flora still maintained that purdah was a curse shadowing the subcontinent.

This was the reformer speaking, but when the writer took over, as she did in *Voices in the Night*, Flora showed a delicate comprehension of the life of which she thoroughly disapproved. She was also fascinated by the interplay of character brought about by the constricted conditions which she so much deplored. She put forth all her powers when describing the domestic warfare between the dissolute prince, Jehan Aziz and his neglected wife. Jehan Aziz, a powerless pensioner of the British Raj, dotes on his own lawfully begotten son, the fragile Sa'adut, but remains on the worst of terms with the boy's mother Noormahal, although their meetings are hedged about with ritual.

"So, while Khadjee sewed and Noormahal cuddled the sleeping Sa'adut as she crouched on another bed, Khodjee (despised spinster twin of Khadjee) dragged out the state carpet—whence all the state and most of the carpet had retired in favour of bare string—set the cushions, prepared the pipe, the sherbet and the hand punkah, lest the master should be fatigued by his condescension; for, to her, all these ceremonies were a sort of sacrament to any intercourse between the sexes, without which it was distinctly improper, and with which it was possible to receive even a scrapegrace with benefit to yourself."

These preparations are for the weekly visit of ceremony paid by Jehan Aziz to the tumbledown house accorded to Noormahal by virtue of her matrimonial status. Together with a rare table emerald, the precarious tenancy is her only material asset. Noormahal, the Nawabin, has an intense hatred for the sneering rake who is her husband, but she would seize any opportunity to manoeuvre him into begetting more children on her still young and beautiful body. Flora explains the marriage tie from an Indian point of view as being not a sentiment but a tangible right, to be insisted on by a wife, however wronged or humiliated, in a manner which to a European woman might appear repulsive.

Noormahal's household lives on the edge of starvation, sometimes depending on the spinning wheel of lame, despised, Aunt Khodjee for the day's food, but the expensive trimmings of the visit of ceremony are still devoutly prepared. Even such a home might be regarded as a refuge, to be accepted with gratitude by the elderly aunts, but it is a prison to its youngest inhabitant, the voluptuous Sobrai Begum. Taking the opportunity to purloin a few pearls from a string which breaks when Jehan Aziz forces Noormahal to surrender it, Sobrai escapes. She feels, rightly, that she is more suited to the life of a courtesan than to confinement in royal poverty.

Sobrai has no hesitation where she should go. In the bazaar there is a brothel presided over by the self-styled Miss Lizzie, jealously proud of the fact that her house is licensed. Her rules are strict, so that Sobrai finds that she has not only disgraced her royal birth by entering the house of ill-fame but exchanged one kind of supervised boredom for another. Born to rebel, Sobrai does at length sneak down from the balconies, where Miss Lizzie immures her staff, to do a dance of seduction before a fascinated young soldier. With a touch of malice, Flora mentions that this private was a restless boy who, better educated than his fellows, had read *Soldiers Three* and the *Arabian Nights*.

It is indicated that *Soldiers Three* has been no true guide as to what he has actually found in India. Indeed the reader is left with the impression that Flora felt both books to be responsible for leading the unhappy private into a ridiculous, if not disastrous, situation. The *Arabian Nights* promise of Sobrai's dance is dispersed by a fraças. Miss Lizzie not only disowns Sobrai, but accuses her of having offered pearls stolen from the Commissioner's wife as a premium to enter the licensed house. Flora seems to wish to make it clear that neither Kipling nor Scheherazade were guides to be trusted in India as she knew it.

From this it will be seen that Flora did not hesitate to pile sub-plot upon main plot, until all boil over in a lurid climax. When the dust settles, the main casualty is the unhappy Chris Davenant, Krishn Davenunda as he had been born. His attempts to Westernize himself have brought him nothing but misery. Flora's own favourite character, a drunken English vagrant has also gone down in a night of riot and arson, but the other English characters find themselves freed from a maze of difficulties. For example, the rather hoydenish Lesley marries a rehabilitated admirer. Together they have conspired to defeat, if not a mutiny, a religious rising against wholly reasonable sanitary precautions.

Lesley is a type to occur more than once in Flora's novels, a healthy moral contrast to the adventuresses and to the languid wives of officials, bemoaning the climate as they drag fretfully through their empty days. The hoyden shows herself to be full of resource at moments of danger, tending to make a suitable match by the end of the book, but it is hard not to feel that Flora, as an artist, had a greater interest in the schemers. She even seems to enjoy herself more fully when sniping at the insular wives, *memsahibs* who regard India as a prison where they are serving a sentence.

The problems that one member's Westernized education would raise in a family of orthodox Hindus, a strand in the plot of *Voices in the Night*, were regarded by Flora as a strong argument against attempts to fuse two opposed cultures. At the end of her life she was still convinced that Thomas Babington Macaulay had made an irreparable mistake in promoting such education, without considering that new wine is apt to burst old bottles. Deeply concerned to study Indian art, literature and handicrafts, Flora could have had little sympathy with the cultural missionary zeal that animated the British in the early years of the nineteenth century. Macaulay was not alone in his wish to infuse higher moral standards in India by way of education. He was only sharing the view of those who promoted the work of the English sculptress Mrs Damer, believing that should her Greek-influenced statues be exported in quantity they would be likely to redeem Indian art from its only too obvious unhealthiness. Mrs Damer's gesture in sending a bust of Nelson to the King of Tanjore would, it is impossible not to feel, have been only a subject for ribaldry in the opinion of Mrs Steel.

Having written a novel on material collected at Lucknow, Flora moved on to another novel, *The Hosts of the Lord*, equally fertile in invention and complicated in plot. Only six months intervened between the publication of the two books, but in both the river of Flora's Indian experience was in full spate. *The Hosts of the Lord* owes much to Flora's recollection of two great religious demonstrations by pilgrims prepared to lose their lives in order to save their souls. Her own struggles to reach the Cave of Amarnath had shown her what the sufferings of pilgrims could be, while she had watched with awe the tension build up during the great gathering at Benares, when the sun was darkened and millions waited to take the plunge into salvation.

Once again there is a question of irrigation, a new system clashing with the supposedly miraculous machinery by which a tank fills at an expected moment. This welling up of the waters is for the benefit of pilgrims on their way to seek redemption in the snowbound Cradle of the Gods. The new canal that causes so much trouble is the project of Eugene Smith, an engineer with a frail elegant wife called Muriel, and the inevitable lisping child. Muriel Smith has a permanent, rather tepid flirtation with Captain Vincent Dering, commander of a troop of Indian cavalry. Additionally, she is admired by Doctor Dillon, the man in charge of the gaol, whose fifteen hundred convicts have laboured on the new cut. Eugene Smith is also the bringer of electric light to the station, an innovation which illuminates the Viceroy's camp when the Queen's deputy arrives to show where power lies.

"And now the sudden strains without of 'God Save the Queen' sent those talking laughing rows to their feet silently, with the proud alacrity so noticeable in India when the act is a confession of faith, indeed! But the mass (of Indians) beyond followed suit obediently, with a starry shiver of diamond-flash, a milky way of pearl-shine; for Eugene Smith's electric light was working like a charm.

"Finally, as if wafted on the full chords, came a small man, with that inevitable look of coming into church which Englishmen consider dignity; possibly because public worship is, really, the only function in which they are not inwardly ashamed of taking part. The great gold chair, the great gold footstool, seemed all too large for everything about their occupant, save the diamond star, the ribbon on his breast. Yet, in a way, the scene gained by his inadequacy when, after a decent pause, a decent silence, he rose to give voice to Empire—in a strong Scotch accent . . ."

This description has been quoted at length because it is obviously drawn from Flora's own experience of a Viceroy's camp. Essentially unawed, she had not hesitated to send in a bill for the hire of her piano, as a riposte for Government's attempt to charge the Steels for domestic services which they had not used. More of Flora's own history was worked into the novel, including Mrs Webster's practice of withdrawing her presence from a naughty child. The garden at Lahore, rich in roses and blood oranges, also makes an appearance in the background of the plot.

Two of the characters, Lancelot Carlyon and Erda, the beautiful "mission lady", engaged to a disposable fiancé, may well have been based on young people Flora had known. Engagements to marry were particularly liable to be upset in India, owing to the scarcity of European brides and the distances which could separate couples. Erda's engagement, a result of her missionary fervour, is clearly doomed to be dissolved when she discovers an affinity with Carlyon.

Invention, on the other hand, must surely have played the largest part in the creation of Laila Bonaventura, descended from an Indian princess and a well-born Italian adventurer. Her guardian, possibly her great-grandfather, an aged Roman Catholic priest, has also a certain air of unreality, but it would be wise to remember the publisher's reader who scoffed at Flora for placing an Episcopalian curate in the West Highlands. He had to suffer the humiliation of learning that, in those parts, Episcopalian curates abounded.

The old priest, Father Ninian, born a Scot, has lived for fifty years in the city of Eshwara. During this time he has managed to salvage a dowry for his ward Laila from the estate of the last Nawab. To many of her Indian kin Laila is seen as an interloper, usurping the position and fortune that should belong to her cousin Roshan Khan. This dashing young man has also outraged the older generation of his family by enlisting in the Indian cavalry. Roshan has risen to the rank of *rissaldar* (Indian officer) in Vincent Dering's troop, but there is no prospect of rising further. Roshan's grandmother, Mumtâza Mahal, proposes that for him to marry Laila would solve all the family problems. Mumtâza Mahal is quite prepared to encourage an overthrow of the Raj, if that should be an obstacle.

Dering, who himself has some native blood, chances by mistake to hold Laila's hand during a failure of the new electric light circuit. This accidental touch of hands causes passions to explode. Dering and Laila embark on a reckless romance, seeing themselves, consciously, as Romeo and Juliet. With the hope that he may marry Laila, still his cousin if European by education, Roshan Khan sends the girl fascinating dresses and jewels from his grandmother's hoards. These she wears to delight Dering, with no thought of Roshan Khan's reaction should he discover what would be to him a descent into whoredom. The discovery, which inevitably takes place, coincides with the climax of a subversive plot, in which a jail break has been planned to synchronize with a riot of pilgrims disappointed at the failure of the miraculous waters to rise.

Vital to the plot are two amphibians, Am-ma and Gu-Gu, river people who can confound higher castes by their knowledge of the intricacies of ancient and modern waterworks. Erda, a medical missionary, has Am-ma under her control, because he believes that she shields his new-born son from evil spirits. Far from denying this superstition, Erda uses her power with a fine lack of scruple. The quaking Am-ma is not only obliged to bring help to the beleaguered British, striving to contain the gaol break, but also to rescue Lance Carlyon.

Lance has managed to restore the machinery of the miracle, but only with the help of the slippery Gu-Gu, who then leaves him to drown. The feelings of Erda and Lance are now so strong, that they agree that it would be less dishonest for them to marry each other than for Erda to marry her unexciting missionary fiancé. The novel ends on a cheerful note, although there have been many casualties, Dering, Laila (shot in mistake for her lover by Roshan Khan), Roshan Khan himself (killed in a duel by Father Ninian), Father Ninian (in the same duel of revenge).

In the general tidying up, Akbar Khan, an eunuch descended from a family entitled to supply *castrati* as guards to the ladies of the palace, manages to secure another kind of guardianship, that of the tomb of Laila and Father Ninian. Also quick to grab an opportunity, Roshan's grandmother, Mumtâza Mahal, seizes this moment of bereavement to petition for an increase of her pension. Ever since the Mutiny she has resented that her pension should be less than that of a neighbour whose husband had been hanged, while her own had merely gone into exile with the Nawab. Bureaucratically, her condition was rated lower on the pension scale than that of the widow of a man hanged for rebellion. To lose a grandson in a mutiny, however abortive, redressed the balance.

This grandmother is one of Flora's most successful portraits of a matriarch who has lost her kingdom but not her passion for ruling by intrigue. Although she might deplore Mumtâza Mahal's struggles to keep up appearances, while ignoring a surrounding squalor whose unhealthiness borders on the lethal, Flora had some sympathy for such a determination to cling to the tatters of grandeur. Actually she showed less sympathy for the style of such ladies as Muriel Smith, wife of the engineer, whose drawing-room, like Mrs Erlton's, might have been transported intact from Surrey, even to a copy of *The Queen* magazine lying on the table.

It is hard not to feel that Father Ninian is not over-romanticised as a character, combining as he does the panache of his Highland ancestry, a dedication to the priesthood, and a past history of a passionate love-affair among the Roman aristocracy. He has also great skill with the foils. Flora's father had been an expert fencer, whose dexterity, not inherited by his sons, had passed to his second daughter. Assured that she had the best wrist in the family, Flora had been fired to practise for hours, lunging devotedly at a mark on the wall. She used her knowledge of fencing effectively in the final duel which polishes off both Roshan, the inadvertent assassin, and Father Ninian, the avenger, by means of a pass with the sinister name of *L'addio del marito*.

The duel takes place on the road to the Cradle of the Gods. Broadmindedly, Father Ninian has mingled religions by leading a procession of Hindu pilgrims. He has the pyx in one hand, his rapier in the other, and the psalm, "*Levavi oculos meos in montes*," on his lips. By a final twist of symbolism, while the duellists thrust and parry, the pyx, token of redemption by sacrifice, stands on a wayside *lingam*, a phallus signifying the eternal regeneration of human life. In the end the two corpses lie among the marigolds left by the pilgrims who have passed that way.

XIV

A Double Ration of Life

Although the two of Flora's novels discussed in the previous chapter were not so popular as *On the Face of the Waters*, her reputation as a redoubtable novelist was not impaired. She enjoyed her position, reasonably enough as it had been achieved by her own exertions, but she had no wish to continue to live a literary life in London. To Henry Steel, whose green fingers ever itched to be sowing and planting, town life with its social round was a misery.

Consequently Flora circulated on her own, her independence resulting in two untrue rumours about her marital status, rumours which were, in fact contradictory. Some thought her to be a widow, the simplest explanation for her solo appearances at parties. On the other hand there were those who believed a man, presumably called Steel, to be, as he claimed, the husband of the best-selling novelist. Flora was obliged to see him off, to use a watch dog metaphor, but unluckily neglected to say how she accomplished what must have been a highly entertaining manoeuvre. It seems that the man concerned was seeking to enrich himself socially by winning invitations, rather than looking for financial profits.

Scotland to Flora had always been the home from which she had set out on her life of adventure. It was also the place to which she most loved to return. Resting happily in the belief that the lease of Dunlugas, their Aberdeenshire tenancy, would run for twenty-one years, the Steels, to their discomfiture, found that they were to be made homeless after seven. Rather surprisingly, their house-hunting ended at Talgarth Hall, near Machynlleth. It seems that they may have been seduced away from Scotland by the beguiling wildness of a North Welsh landscape, seen at its finest in Richard Wilson's painting of Cader Idris.

Neither Steels nor Websters appear to have had any Welsh connections. Indeed, as it turned out, Flora's Celtic background did not assimilate with the Welshness around her. But the garden the Steels made was superlative, beasts and birds flourishing among the flowers. Natural beauty was needed to compensate Flora for a blow that fell on her at a time when she was struggling with the depressions of the menopause. She knew that her daughter Mabel, like the young of all animals, must eventually take her own path in life, but the path she chose was one that had little appeal for her parents.

It had seemed that, after twenty years' labour in India, Henry Steel might have had the chance to enjoy a relaxed life as a reward for his faithful service, with the added pleasure of the company of a daughter from whom he had so often been separated. The family's circumstances were comfortable, Henry's tax-free pension of a thousand a year and Flora's earnings combining, at that date, to allow for the choice of a pleasant home with foreign travel when desired.

Talgarth was, Flora wrote, a place where it was impossible to be unhappy, but in spite of these brave words it was at Talgarth that Flora passed through the only period when her life seemed to lose its savour. The root of the trouble can, perhaps, be traced back to the years in India when she was separated from her child. Flora made the perennially harrowing decision that faced European parents in India, with typical firmness, when Mabel was a year-old infant. That there were two ways of resolving the dilemma does, however, appear in that invaluable compendium *The Complete Indian Housekeeper and Cook*. As has been mentioned earlier, each co-author stated her own point of view, backing it by her own experience.

Grace Gardiner could, and did, boast that she had brought up a large family in India. She had only been to England twice in the course of twenty years, on each occasion her husband and children going with her. In her chapter "On the Hills", she maintained that it was surely better for a husband to send his family away in the hot weather for an absence of a few months, rather than to send them to England which might mean a separation of years. A competent wife, she was convinced, could supervise her husband's comfort at long range. His domestics would perform their duties as they should, in the knowledge that the *memsahib*, like the Almighty, had only temporarily hidden herself in the clouds above.

Although she may not have had Flora's literary talents, Grace Gardiner had the gift of writing concisely, particularly in her directions for moving a household to the hills. Naturally in later editions such modern inventions as railways, or even motor cars, were mentioned.

The original instructions, however, had an irresistible likeness to the song "In the Desert", composed and sung by Michael Flanders and Donald Swann.

> "One camel moves off,
>   A second camel moves off,
>   A third camel moves off,
>   A whole caravan of camels moves off."

Mrs Gardiner actually chose eleven camels as the number necessary for the conveyance to the hills of a *memsahib*, three or four children, and an English nurse. She specified what luggage should be loaded onto each camel. Should a piano be sharing the migration this might be slung in a bullock cart, but, if the road was only negotiable by camels, fourteen to sixteen coolies should be hired. (This is an interesting side-light on how Flora's highly-prized piano made its journeys.) Mrs Gardiner added a warning that breakables were best loaded on mules, the patience of camels being a poetic fiction. Finally, with an attractive cheerfulness, Mrs Gardiner added that, in spite of foresight, there was an element of danger in a journey to the hills which made it more stimulating than a family move to the English seaside.

Descending from the hills, Flora, the co-author, took over, calling the next chapter "In the Plains". Against Mrs Gardiner's twenty years of barely interrupted Indian experience, taking her children to the hills in the hot weather, Mrs Steel played fourteen years of hot weather experience in the plains. She added that putting a husband's claims before those of the children might be a hard choice, but, once made, there was no reason why a European woman should not survive the hot months without undue discomfort. Flora's advice was that a thermantidote, a primitive kind of air-conditioning, should be installed. She defended this machine against medical criticism that it might induce climatic disease. She went so far as to say that the cool, damp air poured out had actually cured the intermittent fever suffered by one of her household. It is to be hoped that it was Henry Steel who was thus rescued from the blight of tertian ague.

Determined that a wife should not desert during the hot weather, Flora recommended that children, if not sent home, should go to the hills in the charge of a nurse or governess. She urged that the wife should then concentrate on making an agreeable home for her husband, avoiding by such efforts the collapse into languid self-pity, which she seems to have thought the main threat to domestic peace as the thermometer rose into the nineties. Neither author offered advice to those double deserters, wives who, having sent their children home, went to the hills themselves. Flora's books show what troubles widows, real or grass, could cause in a society where Englishwomen were rare, but she drew the line at putting into print the moral counsel that she was eager to offer by word of mouth. Neither were hints supplied as to how to handle the vagaries of Government. The housemothers to whom *The Complete Indian Housekeeper and Cook* was dedicated were left to learn official and social deportment from their own experience.

Some hints on the care of young children were confidently given in the earlier editions of *The Complete Indian Housekeeper and Cook*. These were supplied by Grace Gardiner, who at the time felt qualified by experience to offer advice. Two of the children successfully brought up by her methods followed medical careers, which caused them to find their mother's precepts so comically old-fashioned, that she found herself, as a grandmother, re-writing the chapter to allow for modern attitudes.

Mrs Gardiner remained, however, unyielding on the importance of mothers nursing their own babies, or, in case of failure, being grateful to have the deficiency supplied by a native wet-nurse. She added a tart note expressing her shock at the number of protests received, even from missionaries, against the idea of native wet-nurses. It was surely, she wrote, an untenable position to express love for the souls of all mankind, but to find the bodies that housed the souls more repulsive, when it came to feeding their own children, than that of a donkey or a cow.

Time played a more subtle trick on Flora than merely exposing her to the laughter of a younger generation. Having taken Mabel home as a baby, her acquaintance with her own child had been limited to home leaves and to two visits to India. Henry Steel's retirement brought the family together as a unit, but not to an extent that influenced Mabel's plans for her own future. These might be thought to include finding a husband in the lively circle which collected round Flora in whatever continent she happened to be, but, in spite of her intellectual interests, Mabel was to marry elsewhere. However an account of one dinner party has survived at which Flora, with Mabel, appeared in the conventional rôle of a mother chaperoning a daughter.

William Heinemann was the host of the dinner party held in his flat in Whitehall Court. This massive group of buildings has seen many literary encounters, besides possessing a fine view over the Thames Embankment. From here Mrs Steel had watched a procession of motor cars, driven past in triumph to celebrate the abrogation of the law decreeing that a man with a red flag must walk in front of these dangerous monsters. Flora obviously appreciated this actively demonstrated liberation. With her interest in house decoration and her knowledge of Eastern art, she must also have been pleased when Heinemann abandoned the current fashion for crowding rooms with heavy imitations of Oriental furniture. Thrown out with the furniture was a gallery of photographs of actresses, mostly in parts from the plays of Ibsen, for whom Heinemann had an admiration shared by his circle of friends.

This change of style took place under the influence of the painter James McNeill Whistler, to Heinemann both a hero and a dictator of taste. When Whistler sold or gave pictures to the publisher, the latter hastened to hang them in a manner to please the painter, with great benefit to the decoration of the apartment. Whistler was the principal guest at the dinner party attended by Flora and Mabel, as recorded by one of Heinemann's authors, a young married women Mrs C. A Dawson Scott. The other guests were Whistler's future biographers Mr and Mrs Joseph Pennell, Mr and Mrs Edmund Gosse, and besides the two Steels, a lawyer, whose name Mrs Dawson Scott rather ungraciously, could not recall.

It has even been suggested in Flora's family that she would have welcomed William Heinemann as a son-in-law. His age was appropriate, his vitality was enjoyed by many friends, but he had a Punchinello quality which made his frequent pursuit of ladies slightly grotesque. As it happened the dinner party to which Mabel, then in her twenties, accompanied her mother would hardly have furthered any courtship. After dinner, Whistler, seated on a stool in the centre of the company, poured forth the champagne of his conversation Attempts by Gosse to maintain his own conversational reputation by catching the party's ear with a rival story were deftly parried There was no need for Whistler to employ a verbal *addio del marito* Both in strategy and tactics Gosse was completely outclassed.

Any schemes for Mabel's marriage to a promising young man preferably based in England, were soon to be dashed. The girl announced that she intended to wed her first cousin, John Edward Webster, a declaration that was not well received by her parents Flora never seems to have reflected that, in the years when her daughter was separated from her mother and father, male cousins could have become anything except brothers in Mabel's affections Mrs Steel was taken aback, almost stunned, at what seemed to her a prodigal casting off of advantages hardly won.

Having made a distinguished place for herself in the literary world by determination and diligence, it must have seemed to Flora that, in life's game of Snakes and Ladders, she had reached the top of the tallest ladder. It now appeared that Mabel had chosen to slip down the longest snake, with the prospect of beginning married life at the same starting point as her parents. The parallel was exact. Jack Webster had followed his father into the Indian Civil Service, his father being Flora's brother George, who had welcomed the bride to India with a dinner party. From the top of her particular ladder, Flora may well have looked down, to feel unwillingness that her only child should have to undergo the trials that faced the brides to whom *The Complete Indian Housekeeper and Cook* was dedicated. This apprehension can only have reinforced disapproval, felt by both Mabel's parents, against the marriage of first cousins.

Mabel was in her late twenties. With a mother as outspoken as Flora, it is unlikely that she was in the state of innocence claimed for herself by Flora when she began her own married life. Parental objection was indeed forcibly outspoken to the marriage, with its emphasis purely on the grounds of consanguinity, whatever private ambitions may have been disappointed. Little innocence could have survived this setting forth of impediments, but the disagreeableness of Mabel's parents failed to prevent the cousins from marrying and sailing for India in 1900. Mabel Webster felt love and admiration for both her parents, but, having seen her mother's domination of her father, it is possible that she welcomed a change to another continent, where she could develop a life of her own.

For someone whose energy and interest in life was ordinarily unbounded, it is difficult to say that Flora did not spend the next two years in a state of inward sulk. To the guests, grown-ups and children who filled Talgarth, she probably appeared her usual ebullient self. Out of doors she was happiest while pursuing one of Maurice Maeterlinck's innocent pleasures from *The Blue Bird*. She ran barefoot in the dew of the morning to feed the pheasant chicks, who themselves ran over her arms with the same affection that the Ram-streaked squirrels had shown in India. Flora was still, however, in a nervous state, a penalty of her fifty-two years. After a rare literary triumph and a great personal success, the fruits had turned sour. For the moment she let her talent lie fallow.

Mysticism and its by-products had always been congenial to Flora, but, among many oracular sayings gleaned from soothsayers, a warning about her own future had escaped her memory. The prediction had come from an old Brahman, met in the Himalayas at a

117

large picnic for whose organization Flora had been responsible. The Brahman, never before seen or heard of, announced that he would tell the fortunes of the company. Flora, as ever the promoter of entertainment, set him to predict the future for her friends. Nothing unexpected occurred, until he looked at Flora's own hand, from which he read things from her past that she thought were known only to herself. Finally, he made the weird statement that, living a double life, she would commit suicide at the age of a hundred and eight.

Laughter greeted this glimpse into a fantastic future, which faded from Flora's mind for many years. Then, at the age of fifty-four, on a visit to Italy, suddenly the prophecy came back to her. Indisputably she had led a life that could be called double, with her careers in education and as a novelist. It dawned on her that not only did doubling fifty-four make a hundred and eight, but she had, in addition, let herself slip into an intellectual doldrum indistinguishable from suicide. She even went so far as to speculate as to whether the Brahman had not been an emissary from the mystical world whose boundaries, to her, were always fluid.

Be that as it might, Flora promptly pulled up her intellectual socks, and, to change the metaphor, tossed her depression out of the window. The immediate result was a book about animals, whimsically called *A Book of Mortals*. It was a volume particularly inclined towards Angelo, Flora's dachshund, to whom she wrote a farewell poem in the confidence that, somewhere in eternity, they would meet again. At the then formidable price of ten shillings, the handsomely illustrated tribute to the animal world was not a financial success, but Flora felt that a debt for the pleasure given to her by four-legged creatures had been paid. She then turned her attention back to the goings-on of humans.

Not unnaturally, Flora's first book concerned the humans she had studied most closely and the country in which they lived. To provide the text for one of a popular series of illustrated books might seem beneath the dignity of a writer as famous as Flora Annie Steel, but she took such work as she was offered with enthusiasm. Messrs A. & C. Black Ltd. had had the idea of producing what would now be called coffee-table books, both illustration and letterpress to be of a high standard. *India*, a combination of Mortimer Mempes and Flora Annie Steel, first appeared in 1905, but proved to be popular enough to be revised and reprinted at intervals for at least the next eighteen years.

By 1912 the series had stabilized as *Black's Beautiful Books*, at prices

118

that descended from an imposing 20s net, with seventy or more coloured illustrations, to a modest 1s 6d which, with twelve coloured plates, was still good value for money. Husband and wife teams appear to have been popular with the publishers. Sometimes both painted and one wrote, as in the case of Marianne and Adrian Stokes in *Hungary*. Sometimes one painted and one wrote, as happened with Nico Jungman and his wife Beatrice in *Norway*. There was, however, one writer contributing to *Black's Beautiful Books* who to-day stands apart from the others, his later fame making him appear to have been a racehorse harnessed to a milk cart.

The volume *Oxford* had illustrations by the charmingly named John Fulleylove, while the views for *Beautiful Wales* were painted by Robert Fowler, both artists being members of the Royal Institute of Painters in Water-colour. It is obvious that these were painters who had already made some mark in their profession, but the writer who supplied the text was of little renown, struggling by hack work to keep his family, while his poetic genius developed within him. To Edward Thomas, writing in the Bee House high above the village of Steep in Hampshire, *Oxford* and *Beautiful Wales* were more than what he called, "The happiness I fancy fit to dwell in beauty's presence". They were bread and butter.

Among Black's husband and wife teams, Mortimer Mempes and his wife Dorothy were certainly the most prolific. Dorothy Mempes was capable of handling the text for *Brittany* and also for *Venice*, but *India* was clearly a matter for an expert. When Mempes had accomplished seventy-five paintings, it was Mrs Steel who took over the literary composition. She may have enjoyed retracing Indian paths, but she did not hesitate to deal out criticism of her fellow countrymen in the course of her pilgrimage. On the other hand she refrained in her autobiography from giving any opinion of Mempes' rendering of the scenes before which she had herself so often sat down to sketch.

Mempes was an artist of sound architectural draughtsmanship, though he found it difficult to prevent his Indian townscapes from closely resembling each other. In his more ambitious attempts, when he handled colour strongly, he was proportionately more successful. He achieved a vision of glowing orange when he painted Nautch girls at Delhi, rising out of his usual sedateness. Flora ridiculed a man who said he could smell the Bombay bazaar in longitude 68°, three hundred miles from its swarming alleyways. Such an accusation could never be made against the well-swept bazaars painted by Mortimer Mempes.

Flora's character should, by this time, be clear enough for those following her story to expect her to give an opinion on every aspect of all subjects. She tackled the multiplicity of India with the same energy that had gone into her novels. Her condemnation of the corruption which had accompanied the British take-over of power was tempered by respect for the administration afterwards established. Towards later progress she felt less friendly. She reasoned that when the staple diet and normal housing in India was practically identical for rich and poor, differing only in quantity, there was an understanding between classes that had been eroded by Western standards of diet and comfort.

Devoting one chapter to *Women*, and another to *Morals*, Flora blew off some steam about the vulgarity of the young people of England compared with their Indian counterparts. Her claim that, even in what she called "the bad character bazaars", there was seldom any overt display of sexual lures in Indian cities is not entirely borne out by her own novels. There are scenes of public erotic display in *Voices in the Night* which could hardly be more explicit. It was particularly the slap and tickle of frivolous girls wearing Tam-o'Shanters that Flora thought would be considered beyond decency by Indian mothers-in-law, had these descended on London in the same spirit which possessed female British missionaries in the sub-continent.

Three years later, in 1908, Flora brought out a more directly chronological book concerned with India. Published by Routledge, it was given by that firm the title of *India through the Ages*. The author, herself, had suggested another, but on this solitary occasion admitted the change to be an improvement on her own choice. Naturally she covered much of the same Indian ground, but the sub-title *A Popular Picturesque History of Hindustan* was appropriate to a book which contained less brooding on future troubles. Admitting that these troubles might often be the result of excellent intentions, Flora foresaw that they would be deep and long.

She had also been working on the first of her historical novels about the Mughals, which was to appear in the same year. Always devoted to Akbar's grandfather Babar, Flora picked out a favourite anecdote to illustrate his charm, which she inserted in *India through the Ages*. She may have found in the anecdote some reflection of her own views on sensuality. Of his marriage to his first wife Ayesha, Babar wrote, "Shyness almost overcame my affection," adding sadly, "and as my affection decreased my shyness increased."

XV
The Wrongs of Women

It was not only her life as a writer that Flora picked up, she had also developed the keenest interest in the Votes for Women movement, then at its most agitated among the Suffragettes. Widely read and widely travelled, her experience had reinforced her belief that, while she herself could do anything that seemed to her desirable, there were many women still enslaved by circumstances or their own natures. The latter, she had learnt, were often beyond any liberation that she could suggest, but imprisoning circumstances she felt able to attack with the élan that had slashed at the tangle of Government's red tape.

Sex, or her own interpretation of the relationship, continued to haunt Flora when she had left the teeming roof-tops of India behind her. Somewhat hesitantly, she had arrived at a conception of a bi-sexual god, to be reassured by Lewis Nettleship that he, in his brand of mysticism, looked favourably on such a fusion. It was, he pointed out, a belief of infinite antiquity. In a less high-minded moment, Flora pursued the study of sexual matters in the Reading Room of the British Museum. Like many before her, she found that the dictionaries needed no index, falling open at the pages blackened by fingers of previous inquirers.

Apart from her preoccupation with the physical aspects of sex, which she was still interpreting in fictional form at the very end of her life, the bar that kept women from the ballot box struck Flora as illogical, not to say grotesque. Nothing tends to fade with more speed into the mists of history than civil campaigns. Mrs Pankhurst, leader of those who cried "Votes for Women", may still be remembered, but the political climate which made her followers both derided and feared is a lost ice-age. Nor were the enemies of Women's

121

Suffrage to be found only among men who might deplore such daring innovations as the Married Women's Property Act, or even among women who had contentedly led lives circumscribed by the accident of their sex.

An example of a strong opponent of the idea that women might have equal intelligence with men could be found in Doctor James Compton Burnett, father of the novelist Dame Ivy Compton-Burnett, Doctor Compton Burnett, a famous innovator in homoeopathic medicine, spent much of his frenetically active career in attacking what he regarded as outmoded and harmful practices followed by more orthodox medical men. Nevertheless, in 1895, he published a work on *Delicate, Backward, Puny and Stunted Children*, in which he insisted that, while girls might equal or even outstrip boys in their early years, at the onset of puberty girls must inevitably fall behind. This permanent defect in the intellectual race was, he wrote, due to the loss of fluid incidental to menstruation. He threw in as a sop to outraged female pride that procreation brought women "nearer to the Creator's work than anything else under heaven." Only the Almighty, according to Doctor Compton Burnett, could make a New Woman. The doctor was personally satisfied that the Deity had no intention of doing so.

Infinitely far from such medical dicta were the short stories of "Saki" (H. H. Munro). These stories were profoundly sceptical of the moral values which Doctor Compton Burnett had left unquestioned. Sparkling with brutal wit, they became popular with a public overfed on tales of humorous domesticity, but on Votes for Women "Saki" lined up with the scoffers. He wrote a story in which Votes for Women were not merely granted but made compulsory for every conceivable public office, exemption being granted only to invalids or to those able to pay enormous fines. This choking of the cat with cream was effective. In a kind of reverse of the tactics of Lysistrata, women then organized an all-out Weep, which resulted in the Suffrage being withdrawn.

By no means all women with successful public personalities supported the arguments in favour of Women's Suffrage. Gertrude Bell was an example of a distinguished woman who backed the Anti-Suffrage League. As an Alpinist, a Persian scholar and an expert on Middle Eastern Politics, she can have suffered less from the repressions of the past than any late Victorian. Gertrude Bell's attitude shows that, in her fight for the Suffrage, Flora faced high-powered female opposition as well as male prejudice. Her militancy was, however, purely verbal. She had the wits to see that hysterical violence damaged the Suffragettes' claim to be rational beings.

Flora's good sense was not shared by one of the movement's most famous leaders, Mrs Pankhurst's daughter Christabel. She was incensed by a gibe from an unwise politician that the Women's Suffrage Movement lacked the rush of popular feeling which had led to the burning down of Nottingham Castle during the Reform agitation of 1831–32. From the comparative safety of Paris, Christabel Pankhurst wrote to her sister Sylvia, still fighting in the front line in London, that a policy of large-scale arson was now essential. Sylvia felt that such action should be only symbolical, but others were eager for a serious demonstration. By the spring of 1913 enough fires that could be attributed to Suffragettes had been started for the matter to be taken up at an international level.

On May 19th 1913, *The Times* printed three Suffragette stories, one below the other, in the same column on page 3, a position presumably chosen to spare undue emphasis, while avoiding the accusation of suppressing news.

The first paragraph reported that Miss Christabel Pankhurst's headquarters in Paris was likely to be investigated by the French police at the request of their British counterparts. The next news story concerned some cases of arson thought to be attributable to Suffragettes. These appear to have been a mixture of violence and ragging. Houses under construction in Cambridge had definitely been set on fire, but what to-day would be called an incendiary device, found at Eastbourne, turned out to contain nothing more lethal than an old clock and two bananas. The last paragraph briefly mentioned that the writer Flora Annie Steel had been distrained on for the non-payment of rates on a cottage near Aberdovey. A London publisher, *The Times* told its readers, had bought the first lot, a manuscript, for £6, a sum greater than the rates demanded.

It is unlikely that Flora was exactly pleased with this meagre report of what had been to her a stirring demonstration of her own right to vote. She had had strong practical support from William Heinemann, referred to, rather slightingly, as "a London publisher". She always cherished the recollection that he had advanced shoulder to shoulder with his best-seller over a public issue.

The circumstances which brought Flora into association, if only in *The Times*, with militants came from her objection to taxation without representation. If she, owner of a weekend cottage, was considered capable of paying rates and taxes, surely, Flora reasoned, her capabilities might include putting a cross on a piece of paper at an election. Consequently, she refused to respond to the tax-inspector's demand. An order for distraint was then issued, to which Flora reacted with her own form of militancy.

Forbidden to enter her garden, the bailiff held the auction in the market place, decorated, at Flora's instigation, with the Suffragette colours of red and white and green. Pre-sale publicity had brought in an audience of villagers and visitors. The first lot put up for sale had been specially designed to impress upon those present the esteem in which this female writer was held. It consisted of the manuscript of the first chapter of *On the Face of the Waters*. To this was attached a selection of reviews, including one which called the novel more valuable than all the Blue Books ever written on India. William Heinemann made his winning bid amid the delighted laughter of the North Welsh onlookers, ever appreciative of any manoeuvre that can make law enforcement officers look foolish.

Although they enjoy the clever rigging of the auction, other aspects of Flora's behaviour were found less sympathetic by her neighbours. Additionally she herself suffered from a frustration of language unknown to her in the Punjab. There she had found no difficulty in picking up dialects as her husband moved from station to station. So proficient did she become in the vernacular, that, it will be remembered, she had had the offer of being smuggled into a widows' praying at Benares, a ceremony forbidden to Europeans. In her glib, Gaelic reply to the Secretary-to-Government she had shown a grasp of at least one Celtic language. Welsh, however, defeated her, even the correct intonation for "dydd da" remaining, for Flora, unattainable.

With the best of intentions, Flora also made matters awkward for herself on the domestic front. She had already met difficulties with British servants. Their frequent conviction that they knew better than their employer, compared unfavourably with Indian habits of obedience under supervision. The author of the book that had covered all aspects of Indian home-making then evolved a scheme which seemed to its originator to promise benefits to all concerned. Young girls from the slums of London were to be brought in pairs to Talgarth, to be trained in different domestic departments, kitchen, pantry, housemaiding. The girls were aged fourteen or under, because the matrons of institutions in Flora's recruitment areas assured her that by the age of fifteen slum-jungle habits would have become ineradicable. Called canaries on account of their constant chirping, these little girls came to the attention of the local Inspector of Education as being still subject to compulsory schooling.

Probably importing small foreigners from London was regarded as a slight on local labour, for Flora admitted that the scheme was a failure. Her popularity was injured, there being no admiring cheers when Mrs Steel was called before the local Bench for failing to send the canaries to school. No legal penalty was imposed, because the Inspector had failed to examine the girls in question. Had he done so he would have found that the famous educationalist from the Punjab had kept them up to standard by personal tuition.

Although the scheme did not come to good, there was a comic incident, providing a snub to herself, that Flora appreciated. Paying a visit of inspection to the bedroom of one of these embryo maids, Flora found the room in the disorder caused by hasty rising after oversleeping. Obviously the girl had sat up late to finish the paper-bound book which lay beside a burnt-down candle. Inveighing against cheap editions which beguiled from sleep, Flora picked up the volume, to have grounds for complaint cut from under her. The title of that particular cheap edition turned out to be *On the Face of the Waters*.

Failure of a domestic employment scheme did nothing to curb Flora's hospitality. The visitors book at Talgarth was thick with names, including, on one occasion, those of six touring Suffragettes. These were probably not militants, only verbally violent, for Flora was a believer that words furthered a cause more efficiently than blows. She demonstrated this belief in July 1913 by going to London to speak in her capacity of President of the Women Writers Suffrage League.

The occasion was a Pro-Anti Suffrage discussion which was held at the Criterion Restaurant. Dinner preceded speeches by Mrs Flora Annie Steel(pro) and Mrs Humphry Ward(anti). Both sides had wheeled out their big guns, Mrs Humphry Ward, grand-daughter of Doctor Arnold of Rugby, being the tallest intellectual feather in the anti-Suffrage cap. Her novel *Robert Elsmere* had caused a scandal in conventionally religious circles by advocating that the Church of England should dwell less on spiritual qualities and concentrate more strongly on social betterment. She did, however, draw the line at the extension of the franchise.

When the speakers put forward their views, the exchange was polite. Mrs Humphry Ward considered that Women's Suffrage offered the maximum of political danger with a minimum of practical advantage. Flora struck a lighter note, though her assumption was more sweeping. Votes for Women, she said, instead of bringing about the millenium would bring about the salvation of men. The party is reported to have broken up amicably, without any scene such as John Betjeman has described in the chorus of *The 'Varsity Students' Rag*; "I wish you'd seen the rag we had in the Grill Room at the Cri."

The two sons of Mabel and Jack Webster were born at Talgarth, Patrick in 1903, and Neil in 1907. If anything more was needed to reconcile Flora to her daughter's marriage these births accomplished it. With a reversal of an earlier situation, she found herself guardian of her grandsons, while their parents relived her own Indian experiences. The boys found themselves with a grandmother eager to further their activities, particularly when they coincided with those that she had made so much her own when she was a *burra mem*, acting and stage designing.

A supplementary grandson also came into her life through the Steel family's connection with the Nettleships. This was Henry John, the youngest son of Augustus John and his first wife, Ida Nettleship, who had died at the birth of Henry. In the resulting family scuffle the baby had ended up in the care of Edie Nettleship, a cousin of his mother's. He was, in consequence, only a visitor to the picturesque life of hardships and vagabondage which his father led among the broods of his two marriages. These visits must have been the antithesis of those he paid to the Steels, where meals were deliciously regular and Suffragettes the most bohemian elements.

The Nettleship brothers represented to Flora an intellectual excitement which led her into metaphysical speculation. She found Henry and Lewis Nettleship so congenial that, in her memoirs, they were honoured by being given Christian names, a favour denied to many closer kin. Their cousin, Edie Nettleship, was converted to Roman Catholicism during wartime nursing, being moved to take this step from admiration for the faith and stoicism displayed by the Catholic wounded. Her conversion led to Henry John being educated at a Catholic school. For a while he entered a monastery, but then found that his vocation had left him. He returned to the secular life, only to die soon afterwards in a mysterious fall from a cliff. Flora, herself, did not live to see this tragedy, which happened a few years after she had left the world in the confidence of the truth of Lewis Nettleship's words, "There is no room for death".

When he was a boy, Flora had found Henry John sufficiently promising material to make an adaptation of *A Midsummer Night's Dream* in which Henry starred as Oberon, with her grandson Neil Webster as Puck. Readers of *Puck of Pook's Hill* will remember that it was just such an adaptation by the father of Dan and Una which

126

resulted in the Breaking of the Hills. This was a magical contrivance, leading to the children's subsequent adventures back into history. Had such a miracle attended Flora's version, no one would have been more pleased, nor perhaps less surprised, than the adaptor.

Two novels with backgrounds in the British Isles were produced soon after Flora had regained her impetus as a writer. The first of these, *A Sovereign Remedy*, may possibly explain why she never felt the North Welsh to be as sympathetic as she had found the West Highlanders or the Punjabis. The Welsh villagers she describes have a sly independence, with less romance than Flora liked to attribute to the Celts of the West Highlands. She writes with displeasure of the custom that obliged dashing young Welshmen to wear their forelocks in a fringe that appeared to owe its symmetry to curling pins. If her neighbours read her books they may have taken such comments amiss, particularly the account of a carroty-haired girl, whose brick-red face was shaded by a hat trimmed with crimson roses.

Incidents abound in *A Sovereign Remedy*. The story moves to Cornwall, where a shipwreck and a fire in a hotel take place on what might be the cliffs of Tintagel. Returning to Wales, there is a painful episode concerning the burial of a bastard child in unconsecrated ground. This makes a sombre background for a great religious revival led, it turns out, by the mother and father of the dead child. To use an appropriate metaphor, Flora pulls out all the stops when she writes of the wild, nightlong chanting of hymns. The mixture of inspired religion and financial calculation, which animates the minister who leads the revival, gives meaning to the book's title, a golden sovereign then being ordinary currency.

There is a reminiscence of Trollope in the heroine's obstinate refusal to marry the man she undoubtedly loves, but Flora is very much herself when describing the lull of contented pregnancy into which this heroine sinks after marrying a rival suitor. Once again there is a child sacrificed to save the life of a mother, though earlier in the story there is a plethora of mothers who die in childbirth. Another Flora—Flora Thompson—wrote, in *Larkrise to Candleford*, that, in what must have been roughly the last decade of the 19th century, no mother in the hamlet of Larkrise died in childbed. With this example of fact as opposed to fiction, it sometimes seems as if the overall figures of maternal mortality were taken by novelists to justify the creation of as many motherless children as a story might require.

A Sovereign Remedy appeared in 1906. It is interesting to find that, over seventy years ago, one of the characters, brooding on the casualties of the South African War, could be disgusted by what he sees as the modern attitude, "a cheap loaf and a disintegrated empire". The same character, of great wealth inherited by chance, has a painful encounter with the philosophy of the closed shop. He attempts to rationalize works running at a loss, but even making over the means of production to the workers is accepted with an ill grace. A suggestion of a reduced working day of increased productivity is resisted as an underhand attempt to penalize the unskilled and work-shy.

As well as these essays into political economy in the guise of fiction, Flora complains of the increasing removal of responsibilities from parents. Having been an educational organizer, she felt competent to prophesy that free education, often supplemented by free dinners, would lead to the expectation that charity would provide free medical care. This summing-up of the economic and social prospects in the early nineteen hundreds is not one normally produced by historians of the period. If Flora lost sight of the inadequacies of the moment in a wish to point out where some social measures might lead, the problems she foresaw have remained a matter for political and economic argument until the present day.

So brilliant were the bluebells at Talgarth that an otherwise prosaic visitor was inspired to call the smoky blue carpet "the floor of heaven", a phrase Flora uses in *A Sovereign Remedy*. Less poetically, she includes a portrait partly based on her friend and publisher William Heinemann. Generally speaking, it is undesirable to seek for originals of characters in a novelist's work, but in this case the traits are too flamboyant to be ignored. Mr Hirsch is a business man of German-Jewish origin, "with nothing to show his ancestry or his age except a slight foreign lisp, and a still more slight tendency to size below the last button of his waistcoat, a tendency which gave him more concern than it need have done, since it really showed only in profile . . . money stuck to him, and his many kindnesses never interfered with his keen eye for business or beauty".

Later, Mr Hirsch makes an incursion into the life of the more unscrupulous of the two leading male characters. This young man is woken by a knock on his door. "He did not know that the dapper little figure at the door was to him Mephistopheles, that he was about to sell his soul to the devil; but he was vaguely aware of an approaching crisis in his life." The soul is sold, the bargain bringing, inevitably, success followed by tragedy. If Flora wished to make a pretence that she was writing in general terms of a clever business man, she should have refrained from making *sole au vin blanc* the favourite dish of Mr Hirsch, as it was of William Heinemann.

Whatever Heinemann himself may have felt at being represented as Diabolus (as has been said Flora showed signs of preferring this attribution of her work rather than that of Kipling) his relations with his author were unclouded until the day of his death. His only disapproval seems to have been dislike for *A Book of Mortals*. Although Flora maintained that it was a delightful production, she must have been shrewd enough to realize that it would be wise to heed her friend's professional instinct, for she proceeded no farther down the path of poetical whimsy.

The Gift of the Gods, the second novel with a British, or actually a Scottish, setting to be written at Talgarth, has fewer coincidences than *A Sovereign Remedy*, but it is equally rich in drama. It opens with the rescue of a Man from the Sea, in which his rescuer, a laird given to tippling and affairs with local girls, loses his life. His widow, clinging fiercely to an estate that her husband has surreptitiously sold, nurses the Man from the Sea. She eventually marries him after various disagreeables have been overcome, including the persuading of a colony of squatters on an unproductive island that emigration is the only way out of their predicament. Flora's familiarity with the Highland mixture of respect for lairds of ancient lineage with antagonism for methods that might improve the starved land, provides most of the action of the story.

There is a great set-piece of the once-yearly administration of the Sacrament, the Table in the Wilderness being set up among the heather in a pre-Christian atmosphere of feast with sacrifice. As opposed to the intensely musical feeling of the religious revival in *A Sovereign Remedy*, the feelings among the Highlanders that have built up throughout the year are partly moral and partly sartorial. The importance of what is considered to be a wedding garment in which to meet the Saviour looms so large in the mind of the community that it leads, in one case, to death from a stroke. A poor woman is shocked out of life to find that the watch and chain, whose price has enabled her to buy a violet-sprigged gown, were not a miraculous gift from Heaven. They had been stolen by a half-witted girl, whose behaviour is, at times, positively Dostoevskian in raising trouble.

These productive Welsh years were interrupted by a crisis which sent Flora into action with particular energy. By listening to her maternal grandmother's stories she had, as a child, learnt the history of the MacCallum family in Jamaica. Her imagination had been stirred by the idea of the exotic island, which set forth strange delicacies to enliven meals in the villa at Harrow. News now came of a sudden threat to the family estates. The disaster seems to have belonged more to the novels of Jane Austen, where West Indian properties have to be rescued by arduous journeys, than to the days of communication by telegraph and steamship.

The affairs of the Jamaican estates had been supposedly under the control of Flora's brother, James Webster, Sheriff of Lewis and Harris. With a lack of interest that his MacCallum grandfather would certainly have reprobated, he had let matters jog on unsupervised. He believed that the Scottish law, which gave no resident the right to a property until sixty years of unchallenged occupancy had passed, would be binding in Jamaica. That this was a misapprehension became only too clear when the agent, at his death, bequeathed the property to his own family. Shocked, the Websters learnt that Jamaica followed the English practice of allowing such a claim after only twelve years.

Her grandmother had told Flora that she resembled her grandfather. She felt herself to be possessed by his spirit when she set out to salvage the inheritance for which he had laboured. Flora also happened to be the only one of her family able to finance this cutting-out expedition. Confident of the justness of the Webster claim, she sailed for Jamaica by way of New York, taking with her the next heir, a young nephew of twenty-five.

Having budgeted carefully for her expenses, which included representation by an English barrister, Flora and her nephew travelled second class on board the SS *Mauretania*. As a veteran seafarer, Flora found it as comfortable as any first class travel she had known, but her economical category of ticket may have been an element for her poor reception under the Statue of Liberty. Well-known in the United States as a best-selling novelist, Flora had a number of contacts in New York City, where she only proposed to stay for twenty-four hours. Additionally the pilot brought letters on board, pressing hospitality on her before she re-embarked for Jamaica. Her nephew having gone to find a taxi, Flora presented herself, alone, to the doctor in charge of immigration.

The year was 1914, which may have influenced Flora, writing after the First War, to describe this official as having the type of Teutonic appearance suggestive of bad manners. He certainly showed no respect for an elderly female, apparently travelling on her own. Hearing that her age was sixty-seven, he at once condemned her to Ellis Island, where rejects for entry into the land of the free were concentrated. She was, this unwise doctor decided, to be listed as ineligible for a visa as she must be considered to be suffering from senile decay. Letters from prominent citizens were brushed aside. So was a hundred pound note, surely, Flora argued, an adequate amount to bury her should she succumb in the next twenty-four hours. Placatory until this moment, Flora then offered to race the doctor round the quarter-deck, but, obviously aware that he would lose, he refused to modify his insistence in detaining her.

When her nephew returned to her rescue, she had had time to observe the unkind treatment of solitary women endeavouring to pass through the needle's eye of immigration. The doctor must have rued the day when he tangled with Mrs Steel. Expert in the aggressive handling of public relations, Flora at once got in touch with the press. As a result of a telephone call on reaching her hotel, not only was the story of her own ill-treatment splashed on the front pages, but she was able to speak sharply on the way other, less capable, women might find themselves treated on the dockside.

Having sorted matters out in Jamaica, Flora determined to make herself felt on the way home. Before returning through New York, she took the precaution of writing to the British Ambassador in Washington, expressing the hope that insult would not again be offered to her. On the contrary, the red carpet was almost literally unrolled. Escorted by the Captain and the Purser of the ship she proposed to board, Mrs Steel presented herself to an immigration officer obviously hand-picked for charm and good looks.

Surely, this professional passenger-soother said, the distinguished lady would be prepared to forgive an unfortunate mistake. Flora replied that she had no intention of doing so. Even the news that her bad mannered enemy had bolted from his post on hearing that she was due to reappear before him found her implacable. Indeed when another opportunity presented itself to avenge an insult to woman-hood in her person, Flora did not hesitate to take it. Some months later she was invited to respond for the guests at a public dinner. Among those for whom she was required to give thanks to the hosts happened to be the American Ambassador. Called upon to reply to the toast, Mrs Steel rose to apologize for her presumption on speaking on behalf of the representative of a country which had so recently pronounced her to be far gone in senile decay.

XVI

The Historical Novelist

Flora's expedition to Jamaica took place just before she was permanently separated from the bluebells and mountains of Talgarth. If there had been some domestic problems, the place had been cared for as Henry Steel felt a garden and grounds should be. Then the rent was raised, taxes proportionately went up. Moving to a new home, the Steels found themselves almost at once submerged in a cloudburst of war. Regrets at leaving Talgarth were increased by the knowledge that their going had thrown their gardeners out of work, an extra pang being felt by Flora at leaving the grave of the dachshund Angelo. But at Talgarth she had not only written *A Sovereign Remedy* and *The Gift of the Gods*. In the years there she had brought forth two of the four historical novels which might be called her grateful tribute to the Empire of the Mughals.

The choice of *The Garden of Fidelity* as a title for her autobiography was part of this tribute. The Emperor Babar, who had planted a garden of his own, had almost as strong a hold on Flora's imagination as the great John Nicholson. In spite of this admiration, she did not, however, begin her historical novels, as would have been chronologically correct, with a volume devoted to Babar, which must have been confusing for contemporary readers. *A Prince of Dreamers*, published in 1908, is concerned with Akbar, the Great Mughal, in the period when he reigned at Fatehpur Sikri. It was not until 1912 that Flora doubled back on her tracks with *King Errant*. In this novel the fascinating Babar, Akbar's grandfather, moves through adventure and artistic achievement to a death of almost Biblical self-sacrifice, offering his own life in propitiation to the gods to save that of his son Humayun.

Flora's earliest books were drawn from her own Indian experiences,

132

combined with the stories she had heard in the cities and by the village firesides. She then set her creative fantasy to work, with which she fertilized her material, her stories mostly concerning people who, whatever their personal eccentricities, came from ordinary backgrounds. It seems to have been only when she settled down to her research into the origins and events of the Mutiny that she was gripped by the fascination of the great days of the Mughal Empire.

As has been seen, Flora's research for *On the Face of the Waters* was thorough. The weather that prevailed on certain days, the appearance of the historical characters, even their clothes, helped to build up the picture. This respect for history may have appeared pernickety to earlier generations, brought up on Sir Walter Scott's forceful twisting of events to the purposes of his fiction. But to Flora the historical perspective led back no farther than her own childhood, when the Mutiny had been a terrible drama. When she arrived in India the actors were only ten years older than when they had played their parts. Even when she had absorbed twenty years' experience, the Breath that God had sent into the World was far from stilled.

To retreat for three centuries to the days of Akbar might seem a particular risk for a novelist writing in English, but Flora knew that there was a background she could use, where her imagination might work on buildings preserved in their original condition. Akbar, a contemporary of Queen Elizabeth I, was a worthy Asiatic counterpart to that age of European genius. He left a memorial which stands to this day, less damaged by time than many Western palaces. It was this splendid complex of Fatehpur Sikri-Sikri, the City of Victory, that Flora chose for the setting of *A Prince of Dreamers*, tackling the historical novel with the enthusiasm peculiarly her own when faced with a new challenge.

The story of Akbar's reign, his personality and his adventures is so extraordinary that Flora has no difficulty in keeping him in the forefront of her novel. The characters she invents are subsidiary to the Emperor who "was great with the great and lowly with the lowly". She has the advantage not only of being able to use the life of Akbar's court as a stage set. She can contrast its magnificence with the simple approach of the Jesuit missionaries, for whom Akbar's sympathy almost reached the point of his own conversion. Yet another contrast is with the demeanour of the three English adventurers, who bring a letter from Queen Elizabeth asking for the protection of the Invincible Emperor for these her subjects.

To the historical bones of her plot, Flora adds, of her own invention,

133

two flourishing villains, a woman who insists on playing a man's role as bard and champion to the King, together with a courtesan of such grace that there is no predicament, social or religious, out of which she cannot sing and dance herself. Among her clients is Akbar's son, later to be known as Jahangir. After infinite complications of plot, concerning semi-magical jewels, their counterfeits, murders, victorious campaigns, Akbar is left seated among the mountain snows. Below him lies the endless plain of his kingdom, at his feet grow the blue poppies that Flora had once found on Holy Himalaya. Fatehpur Sikri is now a forsaken city of a dream, but there is promise for the future in a grandson of two years old who romps among the flowers. This child will grow up to become Shah Jahan, who ordered the building of the Taj Mahal.

As was often her practice, Flora gave a copy of *King Errant* to Richard Gillies Hardy, for whom she had acted as hostess at Lucknow, and who had first urged her to write. With this in mind, Flora inscribed the book to "R.G.H. the innocent author of my woes". She had come a long way since she had written a dedicatory inscription in *From the Five Rivers* to "the one friend without whom these stories would certainly not have been published". By 1912 the aspirant writer of short stories had turned into a novelist who could confidently manipulate the fortunes of Babar to flesh the skeleton of her historical romance.

Although Babar descended from the two dreaded scourges of Asia, Genghis Khan and Tamberlaine, sacker of Delhi, hereditary traits seem to have cancelled themselves out. The charm of Babar's personality has never been questioned, both from contemporary reports and from his own memoirs. The latter tell not only of the perils of his campaigns, but of his pleasure in scenery, fruit, flowers and the planting of gardens.

The novel *King Errant* begins with Babar's succession as King of Ferghana, a small kingdom lying in Russian Turkestan. It should be emphasized that Muslim descents on India came from the North West, the invaders, with their faces to the south, spilling down into the dusty Punjab. British conquest, by arms and negotiations, went the other way, though the principal attempt to press on through the Khyber led to appalling disaster. The dream of the Punjab was always strong in Babar's mind, though, on achieving the dream, homesickness for the rich and fertile valleys of his original kingdom so wrought on him that, when a melon was brought to him he wept.

With considerable firmness, Flora declared that this book was neither a novel nor a history, but a life of Babar based on his own memoirs, presumably with the understanding that dialogue came from her own imagination. She divided the book into three parts; Seed-Time 1493–1504; Blossom-Time 1504–1511; Fruit-Time 1525–1530. (It may be a helpful parallel in European history to recall that, in the year 1520, two other kings, Henry VIII of England and Francis I of France, met in the magnificence of their youth at the Field of the Cloth of Gold.) The first two parts of *King Errant* are concerned with power struggles for a far from golden road to Samarkand, and for Kabul, ever the springboard into India, but Babar's relationships with his family are not neglected.

Flora went so far as to paint an actual picture of Babar's affectionate closeness to the sister he nicknamed Dearest-One. A frontispiece to *King Errant*, by the author, shows brother and sister dressed and occupied as they are described in the text, though unfortunately any delicacy in the original painting has been lost in reproduction. It was Dearest-One whom Flora represents as sacrificing herself in marriage to an Usbek conqueror, in order that her brother might escape from besieged Samarkand. Dearest-One has already suffered a blow to the heart by the discovery, conveyed delicately by Flora, that Baisanghar, her cousin, whom she loved and who loved her, has early been seduced by a homosexual guardian, making marriage an impossibility. In a short Introduction the author expresses the hope that Babar, who forgave so much, would forgive her for any liberties her imagination might have taken. This forgiveness would naturally include Flora's interpretation of the sad story of Dearest-One, although her assumptions are more occidental than oriental.

The period of Babar's life when he made attempts to invade India coincided with an addiction to wine, drugs being added later to his self-indulgent habits. Nevertheless the dream of conquest was not negatived by his use of alcohol and narcotics. Two victories, the first battle of Panipat and the battle of Kanua, made him Emperor of Delhi, though the achievement of his dream, as happens to so many, brought penalties and disappointments. It is at this stage of Babar's story that Flora's sympathy, always keen, grows personal. She knew enough of the hills to understand the life that Babar described at Kabul or Samarkand, but when the conquering Emperor reached the Punjab she could meet him on his own ground.

Flora had lived in and among the palaces and tombs that marked the flowering of Mughal culture. Her sympathies were usually with the Northmen, rather than with the Rajputs, called Pagans by the invaders from beyond the mountains. She did, however, emphasize Babar's generosity in victory, a generosity which laid the foundation for Akbar's struggle to reconcile Mahomedans and Hindus. There is irony in the fact that the label Mughal should have stuck to Babar and his dynasty. Himself a Barlas Turk, he hated the slit-eyed Mongol hordes who had driven him from his original inheritance.

Affectionate always towards his wives and children, Babar's love does not falter when Humayun, favourite among his sons, is struck by mortal sickness. With an eye on a fabulous diamond, astrologers tell the Emperor that the sacrifice of his most precious possession might save his son's life. Scorning a material sacrifice, Babar offers his own life for Humayun's. God accepts the offer, Babar's own life fading with Humayun's recovery. Babar lies buried at Kabul, where his heart and his best-loved garden had always been. In spite of the tragic episode during the Mutiny when Abool Bakr and his fellow princes were shot nearby, the tomb of Babar's son, Humayun, standing in its garden at Delhi, still has a special power to stir the heart.

The death of Babar brought *King Errant* to a sorrowful end. It was not immediately followed by the next volume of Flora's Mughal sequence. Before tackling another generation of Babar's descendants, she brought out a children's book, *The Adventures of Akbar* illustrated by Byam Shaw, an artist who, unlike Flora, drew with hard outlines and bright colours. She also wrote a novel, *Marmaduke*, which might be called quasi-historical. Mrs Patwardhan classes it as a Novel of British Life, somewhat of an over-simplification.

Marmaduke, published in 1917, deals with a period which might seem history to a new, younger, group of readers, but was, in fact, on the edge of Flora's own childhood. It ends with Marmaduke himself dying in the Crimean War, after a complicated career which includes what can only be called drunken orgies in a Highland castle. These are followed by a marriage which depends for its validity on the fluid nature of Scotch law. Marmaduke's father, a bully of a Scotch baron, is the liveliest character. The reader must suspect that Flora thoroughly enjoyed herself when she was at work on Lord Drummuir's dissipations. There is less conviction when the story moves to the horrors of the Crimea and finally, to the wild grandeurs of the Polish forests. Flora can only have known of these scenes secondhand, the latter being used as a device to turn the supposedly lowly born heroine into a Polish Princess.

William Heinemann's confidence in Flora as a novelist was firmly rooted, for he published not only *Marmaduke* but also *Mistress of Men* in the same month of November 1917. In the latter book Flora returns to the Mughals, with the study of a female character to whom she gives some of her own characteristics, and much of the background of her Indian experience. That Nur Jahan, Light of the World, was the most remarkable woman of her generation, is a fact not disputed by historians. Flora begins *Mistress of Men* with a description of Nur Jahan, new-born, an unwanted girl, being drugged and abandoned under a blanket of sand, while the caravan with her parents moves on. Unlike many of the new-born in Flora's novels this child survives, to achieve a magnificent position of power.

As H. G. Rawlinson has suggested, in his invaluable *Short Cultural History of India*, there is an element of David and Bathsheba in the story of the Emperor Jahangir and his *coup de foudre* for Nur Jahan. The lightning strikes when Jahangir is still in the position of Akbar's favourite heir, precariously so on account of his own dissipated life. He is also already plighted to a Hindu bride, a gesture of religious reconciliation in which Akbar takes more pleasure than the prospective bridegroom. Later Jahangir manages to liquidate Nur Jahan's husband. He thus acquires a brilliant wife, who is also a crack shot, famous for having killed four tigers in quick succession.

Bathsheba, according to Scripture, does not seem to have made much objection to the violent events which made her both a widow and a queen. Nur Jahan seems to have shared Bathsheba's acceptance of an identical situation. Flora deals with any question of squeamishness in taking as a second husband the murderer of a first, by bestowing on Nur Jahan her own self-declared failure ever to have been in love. The perverse cruelties, which Jahangir would suddenly inflict on those helplessly in his power, are ignored, his orgies of drink and drugs being supported with the philosophy that Nur Jahan herself must have shown. Jahangir remains to Flora "the Compleat Lover", with Nur Jahan, Queen of Women, Light of the Home, Light of the World, as a worthy object of his love.

Her fascination with the story had led Flora, in her days as the wife of an Indian Civilian, to pay a visit to the tomb garden by the Ravi river where Nur Jahan had spent her widowhood in prayer and good works. In *L'envoi* to *Mistress of Men*, Flora describes meeting there a Government official. He was comfortably chewing betel, while he watched earth being shifted for a new railway line. He took a cynical view of the reality of Nur Jahan's retirement. At Flora's protest that the Empress had given up ambition after the death of Jahangir, the official sighed solemnly, "'Aurat sab makr wa fareb'. (Women are all deceit and guile.)"

The Builder, the last of Flora's Mughal novels, did not appear until 1928, the year before she died. There is no slackening of her narrative powers, nor of the ingenuity with which she picks out historical characters to exploit. The Builder is Shah Jahan, husband of Mumatz Mahal. (At her death, giving birth to her fourteenth child, her widower built the Taj Mahal, a memorial of love which has yet to be bettered.) Flora finds Shah Jahan less attractive than her earlier heroes, perhaps because she thinks his life of debauch, after the death of Mumatz Mahal, incomprehensible. Like George II, when widowed, Shah Jahan settled for mistresses. In the early pages of *The Builder*, Flora refers to "the smirch of sex", surrender to such sensuality making her frequently impatient. Over the book broods the shadow of the terrible Aurangzeb, who was to be the destroyer of the empire built by the King Errant and the Prince of Dreamers.

Flora's historical novels were written for a grown-up public. Had they been required reading in schools, the pupils would have learnt much valuable Indian history. Even more valuable would have been the windows the novels open on the wonders of the age of the Great Mughals.

XVII

The Queen of Clee Hill

"From Clee to heaven the beacon burns,
The shires have seen it plain,
From north and south the sign returns
And beacons burn again."

It was in celebration of Queen Victoria's Diamond Jubilee that A. E. Housman wrote this much quoted first stanza of *A Shropshire Lad*. Sixteen years later the Steels moved to the house then known as Court o' Hill. Close to Tenbury Wells, it stood on the south flank of Clee Hill itself. The house, built in 1683, still belonged to descendants of the Hill family from which it took its name.

Court o' Hill had an interior rich in Carolean panelling, and among the furniture was a table known to have been in the house from its earliest days. The tradition of hospitality was remarked on by an eighteenth century diarist, who found the house packed to its full capacity. Enjoyment was great, despite a terrifying carriage ride to the top of Clee Hill. Flora, in her time, continued to entertain as she had at Talgarth. If she felt regret for the wild hyacinths, she had a compensation in the view, which laid eight of Housman's coloured counties at her feet.

Climbing to the top of the hill on which her house stood, Flora had an unpleasant surprise which roused all of her lioness spirit. On a piece of blue basalt on the cairn that topped Clee Hill some hand, presumably alien, had scratched "Deutschland über Alles". That this might have been incised as a joke made no difference to Flora. With indignation that made her spelling shaky, she erased the message, superimposing "Rule Brittannia".

Had Flora known that war was so soon to burst on Europe, her choice of a new home in 1913 might have been less determinedly rural. Prospects of a war had of course been discussed for years. Opinions had swung between insisting that the popularity of the German Emperor's intransigence in his own country made war inevitable, to believing that a combination of reason and commercial interest made war impossible.

Flora may be said to have had two straight tips on the subject, neither of which she had received with much seriousness. Twenty years before, a senior army officer, whose views she respected, had assured her that war with Germany was bound to come, but not before 1914, the date at which he judged military matters would come to the boil. More recently a German visitor, a young boy, had been asked, jokingly, to be kind to his hostess should the often threatened invasion take place. It was no joke to this adolescent German. He replied, without a smile, that Cardigan Bay would be too shallow for the purpose of an invasion.

Accustomed to exercising her powers of organization over the schools of an Indian province, Flora was not pleased to find that such experience cut no ice in Salop, her age also being counted against her. This would not, she rightly felt, have been the case in London, where her energy and ability were well-known. Consequently, she could only watch from the sidelines, while the potentialities of women in many jobs, previously done by men, became recognized.

Flora had not been pleased when her offers to help locally had been brushed off, with the advice to go home and knit comforters, but time's revenge arrived in due course. Mabel Webster, unable to travel to India to rejoin her husband, had volunteered for nursing work. She was two hundred miles from home when the Board of Trade put out a circular to the effect that women doing men's work were serving their country as well as if they were in the trenches. Sympathy between mother and daughter resulted in each sending the other a message, telepathic as well as telegraphic, expressing their feelings with the one word, "Victory".

Immediate and decisive reaction to a violent situation had always been a feature of Flora's character. She was remembered by a nephew as descending the staircase in full flight of conversation. Slipping, she gave her forehead an unpleasant gash, from which blood was seen to trickle, to the distress of those waiting at the breakfast table. Not ceasing to expound whatever happened to be her topic, she quickly wrapped a napkin round her head, and settled down before the teapot to pour out for her guests.

Her behaviour on the first Guy Fawkes Day of the 1914 War was equally definite. Possibly the doctor of Teutonic appearance on the dockside at New York had left her with a wish to pay off a personal score. In any case, she gathered the local school children round a bonfire on which the German Kaiser was roasting. They cheered wildly, Flora wrote, when the Emperor's raised sword arm fell into the flames. This effect can only have been the work of Flora's ingenuity.

Bloodthirstiness was far from confined to the children from the village school. Flora's younger grandson, aged seven, expressed a spontaneous wish to be standing beside the Kaiser, with his pistol at the Kaiser's ear. Flora thought that the spirit of the time was perfectly illustrated, when she repeated this story to a chance acquaintance met in the train. This lady, a monument of sober stoutness, listened with admiring approval to little Neil's ambition. "The lamb", was her response.

It would have taken more than a world war to tie Flora down to a private life of knitting. She bought what she called a good magic lantern, with which she illustrated the war lectures she travelled about the countryside to give. She did not say if she included her grandson's wish in her repertoire, but it is hard to believe that her talks were not inspiring, if possibly idiosyncratic. A party of knitters was also organized, its members mostly drawn from among the wives of the Clee Hill quarrymen. This threat to the contours of the Clees increased so much in later years that it was remarked on by the most famous of local sons. Thanks to quarrying, A. E. Housman wrote in the nineteen thirties, Brown Clee would soon cease to be the highest hill in Shropshire.

The setting-up of Women's Institutes in England and Wales turned many voluntary efforts, such as Flora's knitting classes, into groups that were more efficient with a wider range of activities. Flora supported the movement, but she was conscious that she missed the whole-hearted appreciation which was poured out to her by those for whom she had worked in India. This feeling that she was held at arm's length did, however, dissolve on her seventy-fourth birthday, when the countrywomen of Shropshire showed gratitude as heartily and as sensitively as the "little birds" of the Punjab.

On this birthday, seventy-four members of the Clee Women's Institute gathered together to give Flora a tea-party. At this she was presented with a pair of silver candlesticks. Finally she was crowned "Queen of Clee Hill", the crown being a laurel wreath, woven by the clever fingers of an Institute member. With her reverence for Indian wisdom, Flora liked to dwell on Krishna's saying from the Bhagavad-

Gita, "What has been can never cease to be". Her Star of India, although stolen from her, was something that, to her, could never cease to be. In *The Garden of Fidelity*, the dried laurel crown of the "Queen of Clee Hill" joined the memory of the brooch made from the jewels of those whom she had served, and the reality of the dress her scholars had spun for her.

Flora's seventy-fourth birthday took place in 1921, when the problems of peace had begun to replace the agonies of war. The Women's Institute, who had shown their warm feelings for their President, were serious in their attempts to mitigate local problems, although the solemnity of their proceedings weighed on the President herself. Mockery, good-natured or malicious, has failed to undermine the respectable place that the W.I. movement has made for itself in village life during the last sixty years, but undeniably its early days were uncheered by frivolity. It is recorded that, before Blake's *Jerusalem* was, by a stroke of genius, chosen as an anthem, a competition was held with the hope that the movement could produce its own bard. The scheme was abandoned when the entries were found to rise no higher than one which started with the depressing words, "We are a band of earnest women."

Earnest in pursuit of self-improvement, Flora's Institute undeniably was, but there was one occasion when concentration on district nursing and child-welfare gave way to a display of original talent. An exhibition was to be held in London, to which Flora proposed her Institute should send a sample of toys, designed by herself and made from autumn's largesse. Twigs, moss, dried pods and, above all, horse chestnuts were assembled. Not for nothing had Flora earned halfpennies by giving peeps at her "conceits" in her girlhood, the skill remaining with her.

The display that went to London included a rotund Friar Tuck, whose scale may be guessed from the acorn-cup that was his drinking vessel. He was accompanied by an Esquimau of brown moss, ski-ing on the dried pods of runner beans. But the *chef d'oeuvre* of these latter day "conceits" of Miss Flora was a set piece of St George and the Dragon. The knight rode a charger composed of acorns. With a lance tipped by a thorn, he pinioned a superlative dragon made from graded horse chesnuts, his fiery tongue a scarlet rose-hip. Medals for "Imagination" and "Workmanship" were awarded by the expert judges, head toy salesmen from Harrod's and Selfridge's, but the exhibits earned an even more distinguished accolade. Queen Mary, then the Queen Consort, was notorious for a paralyzing shyness which years of public life had been powerless to cure. On her progress, usually unsmiling, round the exhibition the Queen paused when she came to Friar Tuck, the Esquimau, St George and the Dragon. Afterwards it could be boasted that not only had the exhibit won two gold medals for its makers, it had also made Queen Mary laugh.

The Queen of Clee Hill herself is still remembered in the village as a brown-clad figure driving round in a small governess cart. This memory from childhood was perhaps fixed by the sound of the bell which hung round the pony's neck, a tintinnabulation heralding Mrs Steel's own royal progress.

XVIII

The Indian Short Stories

On considering Flora's short stories and the titles she chose for them, the reader must be struck by her fancy for aqueous associations. The sea-lochs of the West Highlands had been a glorious background to her summer holidays. At the age of twenty she was even photographed apparently paddling her own dinghy. Admittedly the background was a studio drop scene, but the confident look on Flora's moon-face as she dipped the oar was typical of her personality throughout her life. Sixty years later the moon was said to have come to resemble a Cox's Orange Pippin, but figuratively the paddle was still firmly grasped in Flora's hand.

Her Indian short stories are particularly full of the sound of river waters. Perhaps from having learnt to swim involuntarily, she had a continuing sympathy for the struggles of river people in their life in and around the implacable force which dealt out both prosperity and death. Beginning with *"Lâl"*, rivers themselves play a vital part in many stories, though *From the Five Rivers* is more concerned with the people who live on the banks.

It is only possible to choose a few examples from each collection of Flora's Indian tales. Her output was prolific, the first volume of collected stories appearing in 1893, the last in 1914. During the same twenty years, she also published more than ten novels, together with a quantity of minor works. The brother who declared that his sister's energy would be an upas tree, shadowing all her life, might now have found reason to modify his judgement, or to concede that the energy of some natures is resistant to upas poison.

Flora often wrote with impatience of English readers who might find repellent the handing over of a scarcely mature girl to an equally young bridegroom. The story "In a Citron Garden" (*From the Five*

144

Rivers) gives as romantic a picture as is possible of this situation, when an espoused pair are unknown to each other. Before her betrothal has been arranged, the bride has yearly collected the blossoms of orange and citron for a distiller to brew and bottle for other brides.

Having indulged in a luscious description of the citron garden, Flora introduces comic relief. Each year the girl's reward for her labours has been a bottle of orange flower water to hoard for her own wedding. The distiller collects bottles without discrimination, or attention to previous contents, nor does the girl object to flagons labelled Genuine Unsweetened Gin, Dry Monopole, Heidsiecker, and Chloric Ether Bitters.

The bride's prospects are wrecked when the bridegroom sees the girl by chance. Although he can hear the noise of his own wedding music in the background, he cannot resist the pursuit of the unknown beauty. He is rewarded for his straying by the fatal bite of a snake, which lies hidden in this citron Garden of Eden. The dying bridegroom achieves an unprofitable union by forcing his unravished bride to witness his death pangs, the only consummation she is to experience before she becomes a widow.

This story, Flora insisted, was true, but others on the themes of arranged marriage, and the long purgatory of widowhood, more probably sprang from her imagination working on a specific situation. The most deeply felt story in her next collection, *The Flower of Forgiveness* is an example of this fusion. A widow, her passionate nature aroused by her dead husband, finds herself in love with her brother-in-law. His jealous, barren wife bullies her sister-in-law, but cannot prevent the affair from leading to the latter's pregnancy. Custom would permit the widow's remarriage to her brother-in-law, a scheme anathema to the wife. The latter arranges another and more prosperous match, defeating the widow's bid to save her reputation.

The story, it should be explained is called "In the House of a Coppersmith", that being the husband's occupation. Set about by warring females, the husband repudiates his mistress's condition. Furious with disowned love, the widow allows the wife to give the betrayer a fatal meal. It is tamarind pulp, kept in a copper vessel which poisons the man who has betrayed in triplicate, wife, sister-in-law, proposed bride.

There is classical justice in the husband being poisoned by the tamarind water with which the widow has been forced to clean the ornaments for the second wedding. A ceremony that would, by giving her lover a virgin bride, have left her to bear a bastard child.

Checking the impulse which might have warned the wife of the lethal brew in the copper pot, the more domestically knowledgeable widow watches the coppersmith poisoned by the chemistry of his own trade.

Besides "Lâl", the first story that Flora sold, *The Flower of Forgiveness* includes a tale with the title "Debt of Honour". A young district officer has a fall. When recovering from concussion, he is tended by an ancient crone, whose feet he finds to have been cut off. Her voice has remained almost unbearably sweet, though he cannot unravel the story of the song which she sings. Finally the district officer's groom explains the tragedy of long ago. Prized for her voice at the court of a *Rani*, the singer escaped death but suffered mutilation by the orders of her mistress. The jealous *Rani* had discovered that the nightingale had attracted not only the *Rani*'s official lover, but a travelling Englishman who, by fair words, was extracting jewels from the *Rani*.

The young district officer has the blue eyes of the long vanished Englishman. He pays the Debt of Honour with a kiss, for which the sweet singer has waited until the very end of life. Powerless in the hands of those who have decided that her hour has come, she is being carried to end her days by enforced immersion in the holy waters of the Ganges. Mrs Patwardhan has defended Mrs Steel from a possible accusation of too free a use of horrors by asserting that Flora never, explicitly, describes a scene of torture. This may well be true, but such stories as "Debt of Honour" do not need explicit details of torture to make the flesh creep.

The title story of *In the Permanent Way*, Flora's third collection, is not among her most flesh-creeping, but, according to her own account, it did have an origin which can only be called psychic. On a wet afternoon in Aberdeenshire, she set the houseparty to play "snookers" (*sic*), while she withdrew to work on a story that had been nagging at her imagination. Whatever the story may have been, it did not get written on that day, for the author became conscious, with her mind's eye, that there was a strange presence in the room, that of a middle-aged man. He was also middle-sized, stoutish, with a red face, corn-coloured beard and clear blue eyes. He introduced himself as Nathaniel James Craddock, an engine driver on the G.P.R. (Great Peninsular Railway). Describing his crumpled white uniform as that of an Indian railway guard, Flora remarked that it was far from clean, with tarnished buttons.

This rather grubby Visitor from the Unknown, dictated a story which Flora took down word for word. At the laying of a line across a sandy waste, an obstruction is caused by a Hindu ascetic, seated in immovable meditation. Although sometimes going on a spree, Craddock has a philosophical tolerance which allows him to become attached to the still figure he calls "Meditations". He arranges that, when the line has been laid, the train should always be halted, so that the ascetic can be moved out of the permanent way. Among the dwellers in the sandy waste the contemplative's precise creed is a matter for dispute. Craddock, himself, thinks of his protegé as a follower of Shiva, the Destroyer, though he, Craddock, leans towards the philosophy of Vishnu Lukshmi, the Preserver.

The narrator of the story tells how Craddock, after a gratifying period of abstinence, goes on a bender which makes him barely capable of keeping his place at his engine's controls. He has, however, the exact moment at which to stop for the removal of "Meditations" fixed in his drunken consciousness. The narrator volunteers to halt the train, but a fall has spoilt the synchronization of the men's watches. The narrator realizes that he is braking two minutes too late, but fails to prevent Craddock's attempt to save "Meditations". The engineer leaps from the engine, the ill-assorted couple perishing together under the wheels.

Although the ghostly visitor had dictated the story directly to Flora, on the plane on which they happened to be in communication, she chose to write it at second, or almost third, hand. This device gives the narrator the opportunity to explain to a companion why the railway trolley, on which the two are riding, has to be dismantled and carried round two squares of cement let into the permanent way. Only a trolley is so handicapped, an engine, with higher clearance, would pass unchecked. After the death of Nathaniel James Craddock and "Meditations", the narrator had ordered the indistinguishably mangled bodies to be buried under the rubble between the rails. When the workers on the line began to make a sectarian quarrel out of the mystery of "Meditations", religious loyalty, the narrator explains that he found the perfect solution. He affixed the *lingam* of Shiva into one square of stucco, and the fossil ammonite, the *salagrama* of Vishnu, into the other, remarking that these memorials covered, in all senses, both roisterer and ascetic.

No such comfort is prepared for the reader of "*On the Second Story*". A Westernized young Brahmin makes a gallant attempt to break from the conventions of his upbringing. He plans to marry a touchingly beautiful child-widow, who sees him as the lover for whom she has prayed to Kali. Against the background of an outbreak of cholera, the story reaches a grisly climax. The young man, his

147

tickets for the elopement in his pocket, finds the head of the girl lying, as a sacrifice, at the feet of Kali, the ever bloodthirsty goddess. When he recovers from fever brought on by the horror, everybody assures him that no such human sacrifice can possibly have occurred. All evidence has been suppressed, except for one garland, clogged with blood dried black. This tells him that the horror was no illusion. His mother, who cherishes the garland, reverently repeats the invocation "Jai Kali Ma", in gratitude to the goddess who accepted the sacrifice and stayed the cholera.

Craddock makes another appearance in this collection. There is ingenuity in the recollection of his youth in the days of the Mutiny, but there are also moments when Craddock comes almost too close to Kipling's story, "Krishna Mulvaney". Disguised as a dead *Maharaj*, Craddock administers justice from the bottom of a well, but his successful impersonation does not prevent *The King's Well* from ending in tragedy.

Tragedy, at a more domestic level, dominates the story which Flora called *The Sorrowful Hour*. Flora more than once took the theme of a well-loved but childless wife who, obeying tradition, accepts that her husband should take another, more fruitful, mate. In *The Sorrowful Hour* the author's imagination created a first wife whose jealousy of the mother of her husband's son becomes uncontrollable. Seeing the child as the enemy which binds her husband to his second wife, she cleverly plants a viper in the family hut, only to repent and rescue the child at the last moment.

A wise woman tells her that there is one other way to win back her husband's love, which is to bear a child of her own. The advice comes with a warning that it is a grave risk for a woman of the first wife's age. Disregarding the evil augury, the unhappily jealous woman reasserts her conjugal rights. She conceives, but dies giving birth to a dead daughter. The second wife, secure in her position as the mother of a live son, can only deride the foolishness of the woman she has supplanted. Having enjoyed the pleasures of love for so long while escaping its penalties, it was surely absurd, says the second wife, to tempt fate by seducing her own husband.

This story is an example of Flora's technique when she wished to throw herself, to the best of her ability, into the minds of Indian people. Aspiring to write from an Indian point of view, she took considerable care to avoid making such moral judgements as might come naturally to a European, bred in traditions of monogamy and the liberty of women to appear in public. In *The Guardianship of God*, her penultimate collection of stories, she sometimes wrote more directly from her own experience, reverting, for example, to the days when she had faced the dietary problems of entertaining the Council of Kasur.

She called one story *The Reformer's Wife*, setting out in it the opposing medical points of view, Eastern and Western, as she later explained them in her autobiography. To Indian minds the solid wholesomeness of plum pudding would force the digestion to beneficial exertion, jelly and sponge cake slipping down with an insidious blandness that would be weakening to the constitution. Flora, it will be remembered, acquiesced, rather against her better judgement, but was rewarded for her tolerance by the failure of an outbreak of cholera to become epidemic. Neither was a sacrifice to Kali needed to halt the sickness.

As a story, *The Reformer's Wife* is one of Flora's less serious sketches, though it ends sardonically with the death of the earnest Reformer. He has been a strong advocate of the lifting of purdah, but has always shrunk from the initial step of publicly unveiling his own wife. After his death, Flora comes to understand his ambivalent attitude. In a country where beauty has a high value, it would have been unbearable, even for a Reformer, to have to unveil a wife aged, pock-marked, and blind in one eye.

The nurseries of Flora's youth had not lacked Indian tales, a popular tear-jerker being *Little Henry and his Bearer* by Mrs Sherwood. Appropriating the title, Mrs Steel wrote a version of her own, displaying a lack of moral censure which might have roused protest from Mrs Sherwood, a strong evangelical. The faithful bearer of Flora's Little Henry, takes annual leave to perform the ritual strangling of those dedicated to the worship of Mai Kali. Henry, a sickly child, learns more than he should from the bearer about the Noose of the Stranglers. The bearer begs in vain that the boy should be sent across the sea, out of reach of Kali's vengeance, nursing Henry having delayed the bearer's annual sacrifice. Finally, the Strangler confesses to the yearly murders which his religion has obliged him to commit.

His object is to be hanged himself within the period required by the goddess, so protecting Henry by an ultimate sacrifice. His employer, the magistrate father of the child, has a vague understanding of the position, but cannot speed the execution. Every day the bearer asks for the date of his own death and how the child fares, to get the doctor's reply, that the day will come soon enough, and that the child is better. At last, told that the hanging will certainly not come on that special day, but still given good news about Little Henry, the bearer completes the sacrifice to Kali. He is found strangled in his own waist cloth. The doctor can only feel relief that he did not deprive the Strangler of his last sacrifice by revealing that the child had died.

One more story of the Mutiny, which Flora included in *The Guardianship of God*, she claimed that Craddock had told her. More probably it came from a sub-conscious wish of Flora's. "*The Most Nailin' Bad Shot in Creation*" might be a projection of its author as an Indian hoyden, though her bad, if determined shooting, would have been untypical of her creator. She is, however, a girl of the same calibre as the woman in *A Prince of Dreamers* who claimed the hereditary right to be bard to the Emperor Akbar.

Another incident from her own experience which Flora fashioned into a short story was the occasion of the mass immersion at Benares, when the sun above was darkened by total eclipse. "*The Squaring of the Gods*" was built on her memory of the young police officer who had had the task of keeping steady the vast concourse of the faithful. He had accomplished this by reporting the progress of the eclipse through a piece of smoked glass. Flora invented a link with the days of the Mutiny to account for the police officer's ability to control a delicately balanced situation.

Having made a deep study of the Mutiny and the characters involved, it is not surprising that Mutiny horrors and heroisms are found coming to the surface in Flora's works, as bubbles rise in sulphur springs. *The Mercy of the Lord* was her final book of Indian short stories. In this she gathered many loose ends together, particularly in one story, *Salt Duty*, from which, except for the long ago rescue of an infant Sonny-Baba, the sombre side of Indian history is excluded. *Salt Duty* was almost a tribute to Imam Khan. It was he who had cooked so faithfully for Flora, while he repeated, without wearying, the saga of taking his murdered master's wife and children to the safety of the hills in the terrible days of May 1857.

Imam Khan, represented under his own name, has come to rest as general factotum to the family of a deceased conservancy engineer. The dead father, partly Eurasian, had been married twice. His widow, of mixed Portuguese and Indian ancestry, besides her own brood, has inherited the daughter of her husband's first marriage, a beautiful girl, somewhat paler than her half-brothers and sisters. The family is established in a run down caravanserai, rent free accommodation given the widow as an addition to her pension.

This picture of a family living a ramshackle life on the edge of the Grand Trunk Road must have been a memory of Flora's first Indian journey as a bride. Too excited to sleep, she had sat all night, her feet hanging out of the carriage window, watching the mysterious new

150

life of the staging posts, built by the Mughals for the refreshment of men, horses and camels.

Having given Imam Khan his real name, Flora did not hesitate to call the family he served by the names that had charmed her among Eurasian school children, Elflida Norma, Horatio Menelaus. There is even an inappropriately named baby Lily, who has come out darker than might have been expected for the child, admittedly posthumous, of a practically white father. With the objectivity that was one of her gifts, Flora describes how Imam Khan's often repeated history of the Mutiny has acquired a soporific effect on the young sons of the family. They habitually sink into slumber before the episode of Imam Khan's own heroism has been reached.

The plot of *Salt Duty* rests on Imam Khan's determination to keep the standards of the slatternly family, in which he finds himself, up to the level he had learnt to respect in the house of, for example, a Lat-Sahib. He has a peculiar contempt for what he thinks of as "black men in sahibs' hats", Eurasians who emphasize the susceptibility to sunstroke derived from white blood by wearing pith helmets even at night-time. Flora supposed that this was a gesture of race consciousness, a theory supported in later years by George Orwell. Two Eurasians in his novel *Burmese Days* are never seen without the helmets that declare their claim to European ancestry.

Although there is some mockery in *Salt Duty*, there is also affection, perhaps more than Flora realised, for the days when she had been a young learner of Indian life. There is poetic feeling in the menu of the lover's feast, which Imam Khan prepares when God has answered his prayer that Elflida Norma may find a suitable husband. The finding takes the form of knocking a young man off his motor bicycle, but Imam Khan subsequently takes matters into his own hands. The story ends with Imam Khan in the happy position of icing Elflida Norma's wedding cake, a spectacle that, at last, gains him an awake and attentive audience for his story of the rescue of Sonny-Baba.

XIX

After 1918

So much has been written about families cut to pieces by the First World War that it can be overlooked that, even from the front line, there were survivors. Some families actually emerged intact, most usually where the men were too old, too young, or reserved in essential services. This happened to be the case with Flora's clan, about which she seems to have been unnecessarily sensitive. The hysteria of the time that derided those in supposedly "Kushi" jobs, as Flora spelt it, caused her to write defensively of the unreason that clouded judgement. Ten years after the Armistice, she put forward the paradox that the women, who had given adulation to fighting men, were now accustomed to the jobs in which they had replaced their heroes. Consequently, they were not anxious to retreat from earning good money outside their homes. Flora was in the anomalous position of advocating women's rights in theory, but disapproving of a practice which might deprive men of employment.

Mrs Steel had not lost what might be called her "bounce", though the organizers of war work in Shropshire had thought her incapable of anything more active than knitting. A skilled dressmaker of the autumn-coloured clothes which she always wore, she did not entirely appreciate a county where modern thought, or fashions, met little encouragement. (At that date, a bride from Yorkshire was even given to understand that her unadventurously styled trousseau was too extremely fashionable to be worn among Salopians.) Flora's coronation as Queen of Clee Hill may have shown her that she was regarded with less reserve than she had been at Talgarth, but at the same time she was conscious that, as a human dynamo, she was under-employed.

This frustration was partly due to the care that Henry Steel, increasingly lame, now needed. To him, Mabel Webster wrote, in a note at the end of *The Garden of Fidelity*, her mother had always been "the one entirely right thing in this world". The doubts each confessed to have felt before their marriage had almost grounded their Indian adventure before its take-off, but once airborne the flight was steady. To expand the metaphor, if Henry Steel sometimes felt he was attached not so much to an aeroplane as to a comet, his devotion remained constant. When his pregnant wife was awaiting her Sorrowful Hour in the hills, he had laid out his ponies so that he could cover the ninety miles that separated them in order to spend Friday to Monday with "the one entirely right thing".

It was not only in India that Hal was prepared to make gallant gestures. Apart from her allergy to mangoes, Flora had a tough constitution, but within it there seems to have been no power by which a sufferer from whooping-cough is self-immunized against further attacks. Five times she succumbed to that most plaguesome of infections, even feeling that eighty years would be no protection should she once again come in contact with a sufferer. Inconveniently, her daughter, aged seven, was smitten during a family holiday in Italy, which had been planned as the climax of a long leave.

Flora was soon whooping away on her own account, so violently that she and Mabel were sent into segregation at a hotel at Viaregio, three hours from Florence where the party of assorted Steels and Websters had been based. The *padrone* was a magnificent cook, apparently unruffled by the whoops of mother and daughter. So impressed was the innkeeper when Henry Steel, ten years married, made the journey from Florence to greet his wife on her birthday, that not only did he procure a vast bouquet wrapped in a lacy frill, but he refused to be paid for the banquets, luncheon and dinner, that he cooked in celebration.

Always the stationary leg of the compass, Henry did not pursue Flora on her high-flying conquests, political or literary. He had never done more than look doubtful when his wife set herself to sort out the matrimonial disputes of her neighbours. Calmly he had watched in amusement from the side lines her David and Goliath struggles with Government. Flora may well have been better suited by such an equable husband than by one with a more ambitious nature. Content to do his duty, to shoot, and to plant gardens, Henry left his wife free to develop the double life which the Brahmin sage had prophesied.

Although she certainly appreciated his quiet charm, Flora's tone, when writing of Henry, is sometimes slightly patronizing. In her novels she was fond of the expression "honest gentleman", when she wished to convey that a character had moral rather than financial virtues. She used the phrase when referring to Henry's face of shock, after an experience as eerie as any his wife's brain could have devised.

Out shooting in Scotland, Hal had stopped to ask for a drink of milk at a shepherd's croft. As he drank, he heard weird cries coming from outside the house, where the shepherd's five children, lunatic from birth, were kept in a pit out of harm's way. Their mother said that they had smelt the milk, which had caused them to raise a plaint. Hal Steel was thoroughly shaken by the discovery of this colony of idiots. He was no less discomposed to find that complacent local opinion held that, if Heaven chose to impose such a burden, it was best that it should fall on a family living remotely.

Understanding and sharing her husband's tastes, they were still insufficient to satisfy Flora's impatience to keep the world moving. No-one could have had less sympathy for detachment from life, best expressed in Lucy Ashton's song from *The Bride of Lammermoor*.

> "Look not thou on beauty's charming
> Sit thou still when kings are arming;
> Taste not when the wine-cup glistens
> Speak not when the people listens
> .¹. . . . .
> Vacant heart and hand and eye
> Easy live and quiet die."

Particularly to Flora was it almost impossible not to speak when the people listened. She owned to finding it an utterly delightful experience. The more people who came to listen, the better she was pleased. Parliamentary elections in the early 1920s gave her opportunities to exercise her oratory, though as a speaker rather than a candidate. She positively relished a rowdy meeting. She quelled one troublesome interrupter by diagnosing him as what would now be called a Welsh Nationalist. From then on, every time she mentioned "Britain", which she did with patriotic frequency, she added, "and gallant little Wales, Mr Jones! we musn't forget gallant little Wales, must we?"

To receive an ovation from fifteen hundred women even before she had begun her speech, cheered her spirits for the moment but not for long. Afterwards she sank into the black depression of one who felt that she had failed to use the gifts that had been given her with the grace that had also been given her. The consciousness that she was carrying out her domestic responsibilities with her usual skill left her with the nagging feeling that kings might be arming and people listening, while she was out of the fight with a voice only to be faintly heard.

However faint Flora's voice might be in public life, it was still speaking out loud and plain in the literary world. Heinemann's six pages of publisher's advertisements for 1919 offered readers W. Somerset Maugham's new novel *The Moon and Sixpence*, which was based on the life of Gauguin. Also advertised were three novels by Israel Zangwill, six by Eden Phillpotts and no fewer than seventeen works by Flora Annie Steel. Friend as she was of William Heinemann, the number of her books still in print must also have been a tribute to their continued popularity. Heinemann himself died the following year, but in 1924 the firm had still a claim to publish what was to be Flora's last novel of Indian life.

The Law of the Threshold returns yet again to the subject of the worship of Kali, which had a peculiar fascination for Flora. The title refers to the practice of printing the blood red hand of Mai Kali on the threshold as a protection from evil spirits by invoking a spirit more powerful than they. In her story *Salt Duty*, Flora had used the name of Hastings for the young Indian Civilian who is knocked off his motor bicycle by Elfrida Norma. A young police officer also bears the name of Hastings, with its implications of past splendour, in *The Law of the Threshold*. This Hastings gets into far worse difficulties than a mere motor bicycle crash. He is only extricated from them by a stiff dose of a drug which keeps him obliterated for two days.

Not for nothing had Flora prescribed doses for the eager population of Kasur, finally herself departing from India in a dream of hashish. For the purposes of her story-telling, she was always willing to believe in magical mystery cures, only revealed to wise ascetics. These usually employ their powers for good, defeating their more sinister brethren, whose aim is earthly dominance rather than ultimate good.

The Law of the Threshold opens with a sacrifice at the Temple of Kali, in a city compounded of the many known to Flora. Blood spurts over the worshippers, who accept it joyfully as a token of salvation. To a young San Franciscan, arrived in India as a representative of the Tantric Order of America, this religious ebullition is more than he can stomach. His vomiting collapse brings him to the notice of the Civil Surgeon. Besides driving a flea-bitten Arab, the Surgeon has other traits in common with Flora's earliest friend in India, the doctor at Ludhiana.

Throughout the novel, the doctor is the *raisonneur*. Such a character is certainly needed to rescue the rest of the cast, not only from their own mistakes, but from the machinations of foreign agents. The latter are controlled by a Russian disguised as a respectable banker, his team including an Anglicized German and a drunken Englishman. Flora enjoyed drawing alcoholic rakes with hearts of gold, this particular bad hat being flamboyantly conceived. Leaving Eton under a cloud unspecified, he has been sent down from Oxford for playing an all too successful practical joke on the Master of his college. It is not entirely clear whether or not he is a double agent, but, being a skilled ventriloquist who can pass as a wild-haired mendicant, he is a valuable assistant to the plot.

Once again Flora tackles the problems of Westernized Indians, who return home to find that time has stood still in their own families. Names can be anglicized, Devi-ditta becomes David Ditter, but the grip of his tribe is unrelenting. Even more painful is the predicament of Maya Day, who, leaving India as a small child, has now returned to preach the Tantric doctrine. Incidentally, Flora seems almost to have had a prevision of the attraction Indian philosophy would have for Californians thirty years after her own day.

Maya's eloquence and beauty have an overwhelming effect on those who might otherwise be gulled into active rebellion. Her advocacy of change by peaceful means makes her unpopular with all other parties concerned, from Bolsheviks to Brahmins. She increases her difficulties by falling in love with Hastings, the handsome young police officer. His English fiancée has only herself to blame for Hastings' reciprocation of Maya's surge of passion. The fiancée combines what can only be called pal-ishness with an awkward shrinking from the idea of any sexual contact.

It takes all the doctor's social adroitness to straighten out the complications. He, himself, is attacked by malaria, as he attempts to gain enlightenment in the Valley of a Thousand Trees. Filled with morphia and hashish, the doctor does achieve a vision of the Self beyond the Self. Later, any joy in this advance towards ultimate truth is shattered by the suspicion that the head of the beautiful Maya has been a sacrifice to Mai Kali, whose worship has dominated the plot. Hastings, safely married to his fiancée and the father of a child, brings his family to a station resembling Kasur. His wife, who must have abandoned her stand-offishness, flinches when she sees the faint red handprint of Kali, placed on the threshold by the aged bearer. The book ends with Mrs Hastings ordering the sweeper to obliterate the crimson mark, whose evil significance she suspects without comprehending.

156

Confident that the thirty years since her last visit to India would have made only surface changes, Flora did make some concessions to modern progress. The Russian agent has a command of radio communications superior to the British equipment. The dress of European girls has become scantier and more revealing, intensifying Maya's problem whether she should be a prophetess in a Paris frock, or an Indian widow in the coarse robes pertaining to that state. The Secretary-to-Government is still dominated by an interfering wife, as was his predecessor in *On the Face of the Waters*. This wife does not concentrate on amateur theatricals, but seeks to entertain any sort of social lion, particularly if they should be Indian lions with paws in East and West.

Political attitudes have also been up-dated, not only by the Russian secret agent giving Bakunin's toast, "To the destruction of law and order, and the unchaining of evil passions". There is also the influence of the Mahatma Gandhi to be considered. What Flora calls "the doyenne of the widows" in a patriarchal Hindu household, expounds the folk-lore that has already built up round the Mahatma.

Redding sahib bahadur (Lord Reading, the then Viceroy) attempts to kill the pestilent ascetic. However, throwing him into the sea, tied in three sacks, has not prevented Gandhi from coming up smiling. Even a firing party has been unable to hit the mark. "Redding sahib desisted, for he saw the mahatma was a god." Her Indian friends and her own daughter may have given Flora modern material on which to work, but she had listened to so many story-tellers in the past that she was able to fit new instances into the primaeval pattern.

This last novel of Indian life appeared towards the end of 1924, when there had been a reshuffling of the hand of cards dealt to Flora by fate. After fifty-six years of marriage, Henry Steel had died in 1923, but not at Court o' Hill, with its view over so many coloured counties. Once again inflation had driven the Steels to look for a less expensive home. They found this at Cheltenham, with the impressive name of Beaufort, but the choice of the town was not dictated by its association with retirement from India. Neil Webster, the younger of her two grandsons, had won a scholarship to Cheltenham College. As he was especially dear to Flora, she was glad to move to where the action in her family might be found.

The feeling that she was on the shelf, a back number, of no account, had grown on Flora ever since her lack of full usefulness, at least in her own eyes, during the 1914–18 War. As she assessed the after-effects of the conflict, she found that these had been particularly disastrous in an area where she had regarded herself as expert, both in

157

theory and practice. Ruling her Indian servants as a benevolent despot, respected by them as the kindly *burra mem*, Flora found domestics in Scotland, England and Wales to be both recalcitrant and lacking in efficiency. In spite of these difficulties, she had never found herself in the position of a discarded employer. She had always been the one to do the dismissing. After 1918 things were depressingly different. Flora, a successful writer on housekeeping and cooking, found herself treated with as little respect as the most helpless, newly-married beginner.

She had always made a mock of the *memsahibs* who were unable to cope with the vagaries of Indian housekeeping. Having grasped the pattern of daily domestic economy, the house-mothers, to whom her first book was dedicated, needed only to spend an hour or so in the supervision of the sanitary precautions, so vital in India, the dispensing of stores and the ordering of meals. That her plan worked to the satisfaction of her own household, may be deduced from the comment of her friend Richard Gillies Hardy, "begetter of all my woes", when she kept house for him in Lucknow. If he had dined out on his own and was asked about the menu, he mostly replied, "Some Filth", which gratified Flora as an indirect compliment to her own catering.

It was all the more galling, in post-war England, to see house-mothers cringing in fear of their servants, and to find that, if she was not reduced to cringing, she was given an exceedingly rough ride. Not only was she abused by a charwoman to whom she had suggested that Mansion Polish might improve the staircase, but the current cook accused her employer of wishing to poison her with chloroform. Flora learnt the sad lesson of ignoring insult. She had cowed *nawabins* and courtesans by incisive words and actions, but she was defeated by the frivolity of girls who, having scamped their work, dressed in shoddy finery to sit in the cinema, clasped in the arms of a boy-friend.

When she was a bride, Flora wrote, her ignorance of sex did not shock her into confusion. She had stared, but she had tried to understand. Approaching her eighties, she may have stared less, but she was still concerned to understand. Perhaps because she had gained perspective from contemplating the gap between East and West, she sometimes showed more sympathy for Indian attitudes, than for those she found to prevail on retiring to her native islands. She did, however, draw the line at a poem she found in a volume written by a Bengali schoolmaster. From the superior level of a Bachelor of Arts, the author praised the simple contentment of the humble coolie, seated outside his reed hut, while his wife affectionately searches his hair for lice.

> "Finding louse a pleasant task
> To the wife must be, I trow."

From her years among proliferating Indian families, it might be expected that Flora's realization of the over-population of the world would have dawned on her while she was still a *burra mem*. In fact, she dated her consciousness of the problem from a day when she was on her way to speak at a function in London. Her train happened to come to a halt on a viaduct, looking down on such a slum jungle as the ones from which she had recruited her unprofitable "canaries". Below her she could see squalid streets, bubbling over with children of all sizes, a spectacle pleasing to a sentimentalist.

To Flora, on the contrary, the scene was a practical demonstration that the human reproductory system had got badly out of hand. The next step was to make her views on the subject known publicly. Feelings of being on the shelf had not eroded her confidence that her opinions were valuable. Particularly she felt them to be so in relation to the future possibilities for women, in a world that had been turned upside down.

Contemplating the situation, she had come nearer than she might have liked to agreeing with Doctor Compton Burnett's dictum that the physical handicaps incidental to puberty disqualified girls from ever equalling men in intellectual effort. Flora did not exactly accept this judgement, but she pointed out that the disturbances of menstruation might almost make a woman into a different person, for one week in four of her youth and early middle age. Men, she thought, did not suffer from such changes of temperament, but she acknowledged that in infancy boys were more nervous and more difficult to rear than girls. Her thoughts on the causes of the subjection of women, she set down in a pamphlet, published at her own expense under the title of *The Fruit of the Tree*.

Except for a Suffragist Society which asked permission to reprint it, Flora was not able to judge if the suggestions on the causes of female subjection, offered in *The Fruit of the Tree*, had had any effect. The title was not, in itself, original to Flora. In the early 1900's, Edith Wharton had brought out a novel of the same name. It dealt with the painful situation of a girl who had married the widower of a friend. Previously she had, for the most merciful reasons, expedited her friend's death, only to find that her husband could not accept her justification for this disposal of his first wife. In due course, Flora was also to produce a novel that came from brooding over the tree whose fruit was the knowledge of good and evil.

While her grandson Neil was at Cheltenham it might be said that a line to the younger generation was still open. When his house produced a short Greek play, which he had written, his grandmother found herself accepted on equal terms as a valuable assistant in painting the scenery. As in the old days, when her white cliffs of Dover had won the applause of Anglo-Indians, distracted for a moment from the dread of the current outbreak of cholera, she once more mounted a ladder, brush in hand. Her efforts to reproduce a Greek temple, using black and white cardboard, were so successful that the boys of Cheltenham College applauded the set as vigorously as had the audience in the Punjab forty years before.

A feeling that she was still in touch with modern times may have caused Flora to set her last novel, *The Curse of Eve*, in the contemporary world. The title, which might have more than one meaning, was applied by the author to the Biblical doom laid on Eve, "that her conception would be multiplied". Most successful are the passages which deal with life in the slums of Chelsea. The characters who inhabit a more prosperous world spend much time attending lectures on social betterment, for reasons that are not entirely clear. Apparently a feeling prevails that the state of their poorer neighbours needs to be improved, which goes with a belief that this may be accomplished by listening to expositions on the need for more houses and fewer children.

Among the most earnestly worried about the increase of the population is a handsome young heiress from the country. To her is given the spectacle of mean streets swarming with babies, which had been an enlightenment to Flora. A comment is added by "a stoutish merry-faced lady, who looked as though she could sit on boards with the greatest comfort", possibly a punning self-portrait of the author. It is this unnamed lady who mentions the setting-up of Welfare Centres. These play their part in the drama of the slum community which lies just off the Embankment, where the hovels and tenements are reminiscent of Tom-All-Alone's in *Bleak House*.

One of the wives, on advice from a clinic, has managed to limit her family to six. She keeps them thriving, even when her husband, a longshoreman, is on strike. Other wives are less scientifically minded, one producing a string of rapidly dying children, another boasting that the only effective contraceptive she knows is a kettle of boiling water poured in the face of the amorously inclined. It seems that Flora herself had doubts as to the efficacy of the advice offered by the

Health Centres. Not only is the longshoreman responsible for yet another pregnancy, but a girl with child is taken, drowned, from the Thames. A visit to a clinic, with a baby and a wedding ring, borrowed to give an air of respectable matronhood, has not given her the protection for which she had hoped.

This disaster is only referred to in passing. More harrowing is the fate of a beautiful young dancer. Having supported her blind mother until the latter's death, she marries a supposedly rich financier. It turns out that not only is his fortune built upon sand, but he has failed to keep his promise not to make his wife pregnant. Even the validity of the marriage seems to be in doubt. Subsequently this heroine gives birth to a still-born child, a theme which Flora introduced into her last novel as she had into her first. She had never seen her own dead baby, but, in *The Curse of Eve*, she uses the description which Hal had given to her of their first child, and which she had cherished in her heart for sixty years.

Flora also gives her own researches into the mysteries of human reproduction to an earnest clergyman. As a result of these studies, the clergyman resigns his curacy. He goes as a missionary to a far country, where, however, it appears that the natives are likely to convert him. He particularly admires their custom of restricting their families by a seasonal mating time, a practice which, the men assure him, is not in the least irksome. Flora's conclusion is that the real Curse of Eve proceeds from a jealous desire to appropriate the male. Her solution is that this could be negatived by an imitation of the reproductory cycle that had been ordained for animals.

For a novel of action there is, perhaps, too much philosophical reflection in *The Curse of Eve*, Flora being anxious to make the points on which she had pondered throughout her grown-up life. The handsome heiress dies just before her wedding, during a midnight ramble round her manor house, where electric light is lethally semi-installed. The death is convenient, as her prospective husband, an illegitimate cousin of partly Indian ancestry, is in thrall to a tough young woman, unlikely to let him escape.

On the lighter side, there is an enjoyable description of the Hall of Delight, scene of the beautiful dancer's performances. The sordid music hall has a proscenium which Flora must surely have observed in real life. "The arms of England, above a medallion of Shakespeare's bust, flanked by small portraits of Lloyd George and Earl Haig, with 'God Save Our England' as a runner below all. Evidently the Hall of Delight was much patronized by disgruntled heroes." Flora, according to herself, was a great waver of the Union Jack when speaking to the listening people, but her artist's sense of comedy took over when she sat down to write.

161

XX

The Gates of Pearl

The Steels' retreat to Cheltenham was not to be the final move of
Flora's ever mobile life. She stayed there while her grandson was still
at the College, but when Jack Webster retired from India the united
family settled at Minchinhampton in the Cotswolds. It was here that
she wrote *The Builder* and *The Curse of Eve*, after which she began to
work on *The Garden of Fidelity*. She had still her painting, to add
pleasure to her life. On a family holiday in Italy, she filled her sketch
books as busily as she had in the days when she had sketched among
the tiger grass in the North West Province.

The Italian lakes were, naturally, more peaceful. She was not
disturbed, as she had been in India, by a wild boar with gleaming
tusks. The pig had stamped his foot, but when Flora took three steps
towards him, he had fled. Thinking the pig to be a coward, she had
felt in no danger, but it is more likely that he knew he had met his
match.

Calling her memoirs *The Garden of Fidelity* was a final gesture of
admiration, even of love, towards the Emperor Babur in his resting
place at Kabul. It is hard to condemn the book for its confusing
structure, for it was left unfinished at Flora's death. There is even a
certain charm in the way that threads of Flora's life disappear for
pages, and then reappear seen in a different light. Unhappily, *The
Garden of Fidelity* was published without an index, which puts a cruel
strain on the reader, and robs the book of much of its historical value.
In addition Flora's decision to limit herself by the bounds of her own
experience gives the book something of the teasing quality of "*Lâl*",
the story which had started her writing career.

In all autobiographies the early years are the easiest for the writer
and the reader. The story grows naturally with the writer's growth.

Every reader, however disparate the circumstances, has climbed the same ladder, from birth to the moment when grown-up life may seem to begin. As she learnt to swim by sudden immersion, so Flora arrived at grown-upness by an equally abrupt plunge into marriage and a strange new country. Until then she tells her story consecutively, with occasional digressions into legends of the West Highlands and Jamaica. There is also excuse for her omission of the names of most of her immediate family. Only a comprehensive genealogical table could have straightened out its ramifications. Helpful as this might have been, Flora would have defeated her own plan for the book had she supplied it.

Flora's arrival in India is the moment at which the course of *The Garden of Fidelity* becomes difficult to follow. At times the sensation grows that the reader has entered not so much a garden as a maze. As in her real garden at Talgarth, Flora plants clumps of the same people, localities and incidents at widely separate places in her story. To change the metaphor, her camera pans and swivels, sometimes dwelling on details, sometimes running rapidly over a scene on which other writers might have spent pages, or even founded a book.

Her Nettleship brother-in-law, while she was in Oxford, introduced her to John Ruskin, Mark Pattison and Walter Pater. True to her decision to keep the famous men she met in their proper places, the only story she tells comes from Pater. When Flora praised the vernal robes of the trees and fields round Oxford, Pater asked her, "Don't you find them almost offensively green?" At the time this had seemed a don's preciosity, but when she made one of her last returns from glittering India, Flora, looking at green grass and red brick, felt she knew what Pater had meant.

Flora, as an author, had always welcomed the idea of voices and influences coming from beyond the prosaic world, while she sat waiting for the spark from heaven to fall. After three appearances, Nathaniel James Craddock seems to have exhausted his repertoire, though Flora would certainly have welcomed his reappearance in his crumpled engine-driver's uniform with another tale of love and death on the G.P.R.

As she looked back over the perspective of years, Flora saw no reason why she should modify her habit of speaking her thoughts out loud or on paper. She reverted with increasing comprehension to Lewis Nettleship's dictum, "There is no room for death". His own death had been an icy one in the Alps, but his memorial was to have his beliefs cherished by Flora. She accepted his idea that hidden rhythms governed human existence, so strong in their movement that brain power could rise to brilliance and fall to moronic level in the space of two hours. Trusting that she was at her perihelion, Flora set her mind to work on the India which she now only knew from newspapers.

She was convinced that a deduction made on her last visit to the sub-continent was still valid. The three evil influences, the law, the pleader and the police, were, especially in the countryside, unabated burdens on the poorer classes. It was the pleader that she picked out as an example of what Kipling called, in another context, "excellent intention that did not turn to good". Educated on English lines, the clever boy of a village would find himself with a degree, but no regular employment. To Flora the education of such pleaders was a sowing of dragon's teeth. The end product could easily advance from showing the village elders the way through the wilderness of the law, to becoming agitators on a national scale, largely from the sight of wrongs they were trying to mitigate.

While blaming extremists for importing the agitating question of a colour bar, among races many of whom were as fair as Englishmen, Flora had ideas of her own on the subject of mixing Asians and Europeans. Still shooting at her former target, she considered that the attempts by Government to staff its services from what were described as natives of India showed a typically obtuse rigidity. On the railways, Flora pointed out, this attitude barred from recruitment many who did not qualify as statutory natives, although born and bred in India.

On the other hand, Flora was anxious that the heirs of Nathaniel James Craddock should not have an easy ride to a post on the G.P.R. by reason of their British origin. Indeed she was insistent that a non-race rule for every post in India should be coupled with a type of English public school education for Indian aspirants, balanced by a far stiffer examination in Indian languages, history and customs for English candidates than then prevailed. Theorists about India, she felt, often overlooked the almost incalculable variety of language. A Bengali would be as much an exile in Madras as any British born clerk newly arrived in India. She drove home this point by reminding her readers that, in Assam, the Mahatma Gandhi could not make a speech without interpretation by the accompanying British official, fluent in local dialects.

Contemplating the system which, it appeared to her, bred agitators, Flora was naturally led to the question of India's progress towards self-government and independence of the Raj. Her opinion may be quoted, ". . . I cannot see how India now can possibly speak for herself. She has many very vocal sons, but she has an imperfect electorate. One also that it is extremely difficult now to amend". Consideration of the electorate brought Flora inevitably back to the position of women. In theory, Indian women were able to vote, but the property qualification acted as a machine of disenfranchisement. Flora estimated that not one in a hundred thousand of the female population owned the amount of property that would, in practice, allow them to take part in an election.

Yet again, Flora put forward thoughts on the Indian attitude towards sex. This was, as ever, to her the flaw in a culture which she felt, in so many ways, to be superior to that in which she had herself been bred. Campaigning came still so naturally to her that she could not rest inactive when she saw pernicious forces at work. Faced by the proliferation of advertisements in Indian newspapers, which promised a carefree sex-life by stressing the ease with which venereal diseases could be cured, Flora collected twenty samples of the most flagrantly mendacious. Although medical advertising was not controlled to the extent now prevailing, no British newspaper would have accepted such socially irresponsible offers of cures as the ones that roused Flora's indignation. The twenty samples were sent to the major English newspapers, and to the Prime Minister, but this effort to shed light on a murky patch of Indian life brought no response.

Acknowledging that Independence for India was bound to come in time, her final word was a plea that due time should be taken. Futile though it may be to wonder what characters from the past would think of events of the present, it is hard not to speculate on how Flora would regard the rise of a woman to be Prime Minister of the Republic of India. Any natural satisfaction at this achievement might not have been sufficient compensation for the setting up of a frontier between Kasur and Ludhiana, scenes of her earliest initiation into Indian life.

One of her last adventures in India may be given as a final example of the spirit in which she met the many demands on her courage and agility. Marshy country to be traversed obliged Flora to mount an elephant. The animal, lent by a local rajah, had arrived without the ladder by which a lady usually reached the summit. As she cricked her neck at the towering side above her, her host firmly announced that she must get up by the tail. This she did, when the elephant had knelt so that she could stand on his hind pads. Grasping the tail, she walked up the grey mountain until she could get a grip of the ropes that secured the saddle. Not having wished to undermine her

confidence, only then did her host tell her that he had never previously seen a woman make such an ascent. He had misjudged the
spirit of his guest. Had the challenge been presented as a feat no woman
had accomplished, it would have been even more to Flora's taste.

Although she spent her last thirty years separated from India, *The
Garden of Fidelity*, with its loving recollections, shows how the
sub-continent still lived in her heart and in her imagination. In camp
she had felt the time of the Mughals to be but the day before
yesterday, merely a few steps back down the long road of Indian
history. Her historical novels were an attempt to repay a debt for the
widening of her spiritual comprehension. This understanding was,
as it happened, present even in her earliest writings. The best of her
short stories, such as *"Lâl"*, *"In the House of a Coppersmith"*, *"In the
Permanent Way"*, are sympathetic to the dilemmas of the characters,
rather than critical of the actions they take to deal with their difficulties.
With the same sympathy, and without mockery, she tackles the
problems of clever, Westernized Indians, split, sometimes absurdly,
between the demands of a modern education and the immemorial
practices of their families.

On the Face of the Waters was indisputably the masterpiece among
her writings about India. Few of the writers who have, in recent
years, made successes with novels concerning the Mutiny can have
failed to find Flora's novel a rich mine in which to quarry. Political
attitudes may have changed, together with the acceptance of a greater
freedom to write explicitly of sexual behaviour, but *On the Face of the
Waters* still holds its own both as history and as fiction. If Flora felt
that India had given her much, she had no reason to be ashamed of
what she gave in return.

Flora's five novels with British backgrounds were inplanted among
her Indian writings, more than thirty years dividing the first from
the last. The shipwrecks, undeclared marriages, house-burnings and
acts of general violence are apt to give the reader a feeling of dizziness.
On the other hand the scenery, the houses, and even the clothes,
come across with as sure a touch as when she wrote of the hills, the
plains and the bazaars of India.

Considering herself as a novelist with a record of good sales, Flora
wrote that her last novel (probably *The Builder*) had sold well. She
added that it might easily be followed by a book that would blast her
reputation, possibly a slight acknowledgement that fashions in fiction
had changed as much as fashions in clothes. With her dressmaker's
eye, she had used the revolution in fashion to good effect, comparing
the wrappings of an Indian widow with the skimpy dresses of the

nineteen-twenties, but it is debatable if she realized the extent to which literary style had also been sheared of surplus material.

Convinced that gifts should never be left undeveloped, Flora felt some regret that she had reached the age of thirty-two in what she chose to call silence, though others might have found the word inappropriate. When Flora began to write she was more advanced in age than many beginners of the same date. A rough idea of her literary contemporaries can be gathered from the back pages of the edition of *On the Face of the Waters* which was published in 1899. Having sold forty-six thousand copies in three years, the novel had handsomely rewarded William Heinemann for the backing of his fancy. Other books advertised to catch the eye of the reader were by Robert Louis Stevenson, Hall Caine, Rudyard Kipling, Henry James and Joseph Conrad, mostly writers younger than herself, but among whom she could, as a best seller, hold her own.

Death had long removed Stevenson, Hall Caine, and James when *The Curse of Eve* appeared in the last year of Flora's life. From among the other books published in 1929, two may be chosen as examples of changes of fashions in fiction. Ernest Hemingway's *A Farewell to Arms* and I. Compton-Burnett's *Brothers and Sisters* were, in their different ways, so remote in style from the novels of Flora Annie Steel that they might have been written in the language of another planet.

Oddly enough, it is the novel by the tough young man from Illinois, rather than that written by the middle-aged Englishwoman, which would translate easily into the language of Mrs Steel. The battles, the love affair, and the dramatic escape of Hemingway's hero are far from remote in circumstance from the adventures through which Flora steers her characters.

On the other hand, except for the suppression of a document that would prevent an incestuous marriage, there are few ingredients in *Brothers and Sisters* which would not curdle like mayonnaise if dropped into one of Flora's mixtures. As well as a *penchant* for the possibilities of incestuous situations, I. Compton-Burnett has a special line in domestic tyrants. Here alone Flora may be said to have something in common with the later novelist, which enables her to paint strong portraits of Indian matriarchs. Except for its occurrence among the families of the Mughals, Flora, like Professor Gilbert Murray, was only interested in incest in a general sort of way. Violence, in her novels, usually taking place on stage, Flora's characters are too busy picking up the pieces to think about the immediate effect upon themselves in the Compton-Burnett manner.

For the composition of *The Curse of Eve*, Flora made notes mostly incorporated into the story, though some, unused, were found among her papers after her death. These notes included two quotations from Frazer's *Golden Bough* about "the deep ingrained dread" felt by man for the power of woman, together with a comment from the scientist Metchnikoff that, "The sex functions in man are the greatest disharmony in nature". It is fair to say that on these two points Flora would have been likely to have found more sympathy from Ivy Compton-Burnett than from Ernest Hemingway.

According to her daughter's account of the last two years of Flora's life, she had been immobilized by an abrasion which resisted treatment. Suddenly, her resilience swept away the trouble, with the completeness of a magical cure such as had come to young Hastings in *The Law of the Threshold*. With the support of her grandson Neil, she once again sailed for Jamaica. He has recorded that, on the voyage, she was the life and soul of the Captain's table. Her progress round the family property and the island was a triumph, but she still did not allow her enjoyment to halt her determination to spread her views. Back at home, she wrote so strongly of her West Indian experiences that a discussion started in the Press, on the then important, if now obsolete, subject of Empire Free Trade.

Time and space had become a preoccupation, a matter for further study. Still with her memories of Lewis Nettleship and his insistence that there was "no room for death", Flora joined her grandson Neil in his rooms at Oxford. Here she read daily in the Bodleian, an attempt to keep term rare among octogenarians. More than once she had written that all the elements were, after all, the Lord's, so that human beings might well pass into them in a glorious evaporation, a possibility that led her to regard the diminishing future with calmness.

One of her great-nephews has preserved a manuscript adaptation headed "Last Wishes". The adaptation is based on the hymn,

> "O strength and stay
> Upholding all creation,"

which the *English Hymnal* attributes to St Ambrose. Evidently Flora felt that St Ambrose had not entirely covered the situation. Although she left the first verse unaltered, and only changed the final two lines of the last verse, she interposed an original verse between:

> "Into Thy hands myself I give, well witting
> Mistake can ne'er be thine, Oh wise and true,
> Make me whate'er Thy Great World Plan deems fitting,
> Do with me what Thy Wisdom wills to do."

Having composed her curtain speech, Flora continued her performance in the production she had made so very much her own. In writing *The Garden of Fidelity* she had reached the point where it would have been necessary to speak of the death of her husband. Here she broke off, leaving a sentence on the subject of ordinary comprehension of the Derating Bill in mid-air. She may have wished to pause before writing about how she faced life as a widow. Instead, she picked up a tale which, like so many in the past, had long been simmering at the back of her mind.

If there had been some reserve between herself and the native Welsh in her years at Talgarth, it had melted when she returned with a reading party of her grandson's. Her welcome was of the warmest, while the beauty round her was immutable. It was here that she spent her eighty-second birthday, among scenes which had been the background of what she had called the "Suffrage Years". If she regarded the new generation as thoughtless inheritors of their elders' victory, she did not allow disillusion to darken her sky.

Her daughter's words can best describe Flora's last step towards the snow-topped mountains to which her eyes had been lifted up increasingly as the years passed. Mabel Webster wrote: "She turned from her *Garden of Fidelity* to a tale planned long ago, *The Gates of Pearl*, and while telling of those who sought them, suddenly and splendidly passed within them".

Flora died on April 12th, 1929 ten days after she had celebrated her birthday among places that had held so much delight, and had been the home of many of her writing years. At her death, her novel of the Mutiny was still in print, but shortly afterwards there was to be a critical eclipse, blotting out the works of Kipling and other writers whose views on India were considered old-fashioned. While Kipling began to be restored in reputation within less than twenty years, it took considerably longer for the days of the Raj to be seen in perspective and to regain literary popularity. *On the Face of the Waters*, a victim of this swing in fashion, has yet to be re-established as a seminal work in its own field, even though the pendulum has swung in the opposite direction. Nothing can, however, rob the book of an epic quality, a firm historical foundation and an understanding of the Breath which God sent into the World.

At the time of the scandal in the University of the Punjab, Flora had been infinitely touched by the devotion of her scholars. They had showed their affection by sitting up all night, spinning thread which was then woven into cloth to be made into a dress. Flora had always determined that she would wear this dress when her end

169

came, even taking the precaution of packing it on her journey to Jamaica, in case death might overtake her far from home. So, in due course, she was cremated in a shroud spun by the loving hands of the "little birds", schoolgirls at Lahore. She had, long ago, made up her mind that she wished to disappear into thin air, "which is the Lord's also". Surrounded by those dearest to her, she did indeed so disappear.

Flora Annie Steel cannot be left with a better epitaph than the proverb quoted by the Emperor Babar, her most loved of the Mughals: "Death in the company of friends is a feast."

Index